Regain control of your life
Counsel to ease your anxiety

Patrick Baron

GeniusMedia
CREATING KNOWLEDGE

2023

Regain control of your life

Counsel to ease your anxiety

First Edition: January 2023

ISBN 978-1-908293-61-9

Genius Media 2023

© Patrick Baron 2021

Genius Media

B1502

PO Box 15113

Birmingham

B2 2NJ

www.geniusmedia.pub

books@geniusmedia.pub

Contents

Introduction

It is interesting that although I wrote this book a year before the Coronavirus crisis, a lot of people have been forced to experience what I described in this book: to slow down, to consider oneself and what matters, to learn to accept and to be present in their life, their aspirations, or lack of them. Some have been able to deal with these changes positively, creatively, and constructively. The pandemic allowed a readjustment of life's priorities and direction. However, this period also became a source of anxiety and stress for others, who realised they were in a rut and unable to react in the right way.

The aim of many psychological therapies is to raise awareness of your actions and habits, and to understand your not so useful patterns. Learning and change starts with a realisation. Something you had not realised before, had not been paying attention to. With perspective, you can disrupt the pattern and learn a better way to deal with the situation. At the end of each chapter of this book, there are tasks that are designed to raise your awareness. When awareness increases, the changes you can make to improve your life should become more evident. You will need to fight the temptation to find a quick solution. The intention is to help you recognise, accept, and acknowledge the patterns that cause anxiety and what steps can be taken to overcome them.

When I work with a client, we start with their problem. We examine it to understand how the problem works. We develop alternative solutions. What matters is that they develop a new mindset to prevent the issue from reoccurring. The client regains control of their life.

This book follows the same format. It is mainly about understanding the mechanics of anxiety. The behaviours people develop to compensate for the feeling of anxiety and how to turn bad habits into good habits. The text, like the therapeutic process, goes from problem to solution.

You will discover how anxiety works, how you get stressed, become reactive and hopeless. You will explore how, to feel better, we engage in habitual activities to move away from those bad feelings. We will examine coping mechanisms and how some of these activities are constructive and socially acceptable: helping others, creative hobbies, and even burying oneself in work. Whilst other activities can make things worse, like binging, shopping, drugs and alcohol, mindless television, or losing oneself on addictive sites and apps. We will then address how we respond, justify and deal with those activities unconsciously to bring stability to our lives, feel better and prevent further suffering.

Regain control of your life will address various aspects of the situation, provide explanations and examples you can relate to, and show you solutions to escape unhelpful patterns, regain control and advance in life with confidence. Reading this book all at once would convince you that it makes sense, but re-reading it and working on one idea at a time is a more natural way to progress. In life, you don't learn everything at once. Every day you learn, grow your awareness, and update your system.

When you read the chapters, you may wonder: Does it apply to my life? The information is helpful, but so what? So at the end of each chapter, there is an exercise you can do to help you integrate and apply your learning.

A word of caution

When you were feeling low as a child, your parents fulfilled your needs. Consequently, when you feel needy as an adult, there is a natural tendency to look for something outside yourself to rescue you, meet your demands, and fulfil your needs. If you feel bad, maybe the solution is in a book, including this one. Perhaps retail therapy or displaced activities, such as switching on the TV, eating biscuits, and checking Facebook, do the trick. However, these patterns are unreliable and would generate anxiety and powerlessness. You may become passive-aggressive, find another activity to escape, or become angry and complain. As you are reading this book, you may experience the same thing. You may hope there is a simple formula that will solve it all. You may have read many books and articles that try to break it down into a simple recipe. Yet it didn't work. So you are still searching, probably half-heartedly, hoping to find the solution. I would encourage you to stay with it. Be patient, read, reflect and learn.

As you are not able to deal with the sources of anxiety, they can remain buried in your subconscious. Keeping them there is an in-built safety mechanism, but as you become more in control and more confident, you should be able to start to see what was hidden up till then. The more capable you become at dealing with your anxiety, the more likely that buried issues will surface. On the positive side, it means that you are now more ready to deal with them, and more opportunities to move forward with confidence will appear.

Acknowledgements

Most of what is written comes from observation, life, work with clients, and discussions with my friend and fellow psychotherapist, Kieron Deahl. We studied NLP and Developmental Behavioural Modelling 30 years ago. Since

Regain control of your life

then, we have had regular meetings to discuss the ideas we came up with, with the fervour of driven alchemists.

On my path, I have met many people who have been instrumental in stimulating, nourishing, and supporting my thoughts and model. I would like to thank all my friends in the NLP world, particularly John McWhirter, Fran Burgess, Derek Jackson, Judith Lowe, and Peter Freeth. And countless others that are too many to list.

Thanks to Tamara Russell and Maimuna May for their proofreading contributions.

I rarely refer to others' work, referring to concepts and ideas that others had written about, as this is not an academic book. It is one based on my experience and reflections. I have not read books on anxiety because I have plenty of material by analysing how my and others' anxiety works. I have, however, mentioned some approaches that I have come across and found interesting.

About anxiety

You have anxiety, don't know what's going to happen, and feel there is a danger in not knowing. This perceived imminent danger may worsen. You don't know how, but you know it is real. For example, you are overwhelmed as you cannot keep up with the demand, and it ends up being too much. You stress. The implications of not being able to cope may be that people will reject you, or you are about to cry, and all the attention will be on you.

They say that nature does not like a vacuum, and it's the same for human nature. We must fill the void of uncertainty. Trauma victims escape an unpleasant reality by letting their minds go into other realities. Companies behave like humans; they don't like uncertainty. They plan what will happen in as much detail as possible. They divide up the responsibilities. They have risk registers to think about what could go wrong and what to do if it happens. They have project management tools.

You could do the same. To fight anxiety, use that feeling as a prompt to react and create a plan. First, you need to clarify what is going on and what to do. Then you need to consider the dangers and how to counter them.

It is the simplest and most direct action against anxiety. Yet the human mind is such that it is difficult. Here's why: all anxiety has a common pattern: a thought or a picture, out of awareness, has negative implications and means you are not in control. Because it makes you tense and insecure, you don't think the thought through rationally, and you don't engage with it.

Now you have a relationship between you and your tension. That tension tells you that you are not in control. You feel bad. Why do you feel bad? You don't know because you don't have actual evidence, but you know that you feel tense, that is real, so you search for the evidence that causes you to dread, which locks the feeling in place. You may be aware of the context or the situation but not its implications. For example, the spider could attack you, but you don't think through what would happen if it did. It is the absence of this conclusion that causes you to feel dread. So you supply one, trapping yourself in a system of cause and effect.

There are many forms of anxiety, described amongst others as Generalised Anxiety Disorder, Social Phobias, and other phobias, such as Obsessive Compulsive Disorder, Panic Disorder, and Post Traumatic Stress Disorder.

In the context of relationship anxiety, you would know that it is about your partner maybe leaving you or doing something behind your back. That would jeopardise trust. You may have a negative mental picture of them being with another person, which may make you feel jealous, or a picture of yourself alone and sad. So whenever they are out of sight, with someone else, or they may even be in front of you, the idea that they could betray you would flash in your mind, and you would tense. That tension would be your cue for feeling validated in feeling that you can't trust them. You would then feed evidence for feeling bad by fantasising with thoughts or scenarios of betrayal. You would feed your suspicion and may even know that you are making it up, but at least you would focus on something rather than feeling bad and not knowing why. The next stage would be acting in reality, such as monitoring texts on their phone or investigating their whereabouts. You would then justify your actions by convincing yourself that you can't trust them.

In the context of social anxiety, such as having to speak or perform in public or doing a presentation at work, one would become highly self-conscious and experience very negative feelings of being judged and making a fool of themselves. It could cause sweating, blushing, and stuttering. There is an element of not being capable but also being humiliated, embarrassed, and ostracised.

There is also agoraphobia, the fear of being in a space where something could happen and not being able to escape, or the opposite, getting lost. Again, the thought of it would increase a feeling of losing control and could lead to a panic attack.

These three examples have the same structure as I described in the generalised pattern above. So I will not address the different forms in this book, although I will be giving examples to illustrate the components.

Adding to what I have described, what exacerbates and makes anxiety more potent is that people blame themselves; they ruminate on this and find more evidence to lock in the fact that they are anxious.

Additionally, when they avoid confronting the reality of their fear, there is a sense of relief, as it reinforces avoidance and reinforces the vicious circle.

Chapters in the book

Allow me to share a brief overview of the structure of the book before getting into the details.

Life is stressful

Whatever the circumstances, everyone is wondering about the context of their lives. It may be in the moment or their whole lives. We are all on a continuum of relaxation/stress, depending on how we perceive the world around us.

Stress

Stress affects your state. When you feel stressed and not in control, you become anxious. Therefore, you become hyper-vigilant about what could go wrong. As a result, you become overwhelmed and consequently even less in control. It becomes a vicious circle.

Resources and demands

When we think of the demand and resources in a situation, they appear static. In practice, it isn't. They are constantly influencing each other. To be able to think of a situation and evaluate risks and benefits, we need to work with ideas and facts which are fixed. In reality, everything is in constant flow. When the demands increase, the resources are affected. When the resources increase, the demand doesn't appear as much of a big deal.

Domination

The unwanted demands of a situation make you feel dominated by it, as you feel forced to do or experience something you don't want. You are often unaware of it happening, whether it is imposed by others or yourself. It can make you feel like a victim of the situation against which you react.

Hopelessness and control

You were not in control of your life in the past. You are not now. It causes you to think you won't be in control in the future either. The feeling of hopelessness reinforces itself through searching and finding evidence of hopelessness.

Passivity and belonging

When we don't feel we belong, we become passive. We long to be rescued or escape in comforting activities, like going for a walk, eating cake, or drinking. It's a form of trance.

Tension and reaction

The more stressed you are, the more tense you are, and consequently, the more reactive you become. You have no choice. You defend yourself.

Deciding

The decision process in itself produces tension. It is connected to the fear of missing out. What if it is the wrong choice? What are the consequences? We don't know so we shy away from the process of deciding.

Prediction

The whole process of life, even for simple life forms, is to predict the interaction with the environment (e.g. others, events, life). Figuring out what will happen, whether it will be good, bad, friendly, or hostile, prepares us to seek or avoid situations. Not knowing what will happen next means you are on a slippery slope that you don't control. To predict, we need some certainty.

Integrity

Now you also know that you can't count on yourself, as you can't decide or commit. You don't do what you say you would do, so you are unreliable. You have to live with it.

The behaviours we engage in to avoid anxiety

Purpose, goals, and projects can be considered as distractions from the angst of being directionless and purposeless. They are coping mechanisms. Distractions can be for a moment or last a lifetime, and they can also be socially acceptable or disapproved.

Having a 'to-do'

When you have a task you don't want to do, a distraction takes you away from it. The more urgent the demand of the unwanted obligation, the more urgent the need to escape its domination with a something that will keep your attention elsewhere.

Not thinking

Because it is in the context of problem-solving, thinking in itself creates tension. Therefore, we don't think.

Background / foreground

If these two are aligned, you would feel good. Generally, the background is the purpose, the context, and the foreground is what is happening here and now.

If you focus on the foreground, then the background, but not simultaneously, you will somehow feel guilty or ashamed about wasting time or being unable to control an addiction.

After alignment, the next dynamic is ensuring the focus is clear.

Different levels

Any action or thinking operates at different levels. Some are aligned, and others conflict. It leads to damned if you do, damned if you don't.

The solution is the problem

Often the wrong solution reinforces and even compounds the problem. But having a solution feels good, and we become attached to it because we have come up with it.

You are cursed – the stories you tell yourself

Applying a solution that doesn't work will reinforce the initial conviction that something is wrong with you. Despite this, people do things just to deny that there is something wrong, but they know, and it is hopeless.

Is there hope, Doctor?

Controlling the environment

Because we don't have control over many things in life, we create the environment and conditions to have more control over what will happen in the future. Humanity has done that throughout history.

I believe

We control our moral environment with our beliefs. In that environment, we feel at home. We belong. Whatever doesn't fit is rejected, especially when we are stressed.

Because we can

People are often driven to do things because they can, rather than it being meaningful. The reasons are often unconscious and reactive. It is programming led by ego.

On automatic pilot

Most of what we do is unconscious. It is said that 99% of what we do is operating out of habit. The process of doing something has been established through practice. We don't need to think about it. But we can regain control over what is automatic and not useful.

The 'can mode'

In the 'can mode', there are three aspects: availability, permission, and pleasure. Those components are unconsciously present and intertwined in an unconscious habit. So when you go from consciously incompetent to unconsciously competent, you are in the 'can mode'.

In the 'meaning mode'

Things are not just as they are. Meaning is found everywhere, in semantics, symbols, or culture. You get upset when meanings are not respected. You can't help but attribute meaning.

'Is' and 'should be'

We are constantly comparing what 'is' and what 'should be'. How do you know what 'is'? How do you know what 'should be'? What is the relationship between the two?

Map and territory

Map and territory is a useful analogy in explaining what's happening in the mind. What is happening now is the territory, and what should be happening is the map.

What is happening between 'is' and 'should be'?

Where there is a discrepancy between what 'should be' and what 'is', there is tension and energy. The reaction to this discrepancy, if unwanted, is often expressed by the five stages of grief: denial, anger, bargaining, depression, and acceptance.

So what?

When you listen to someone's emotions, you can hear all the implied shoulds and should nots. For example, when somebody is angry or sad, things are not as they should be.

When your mood, attitude and frame of mind are negative, they are indicative of the relationship between what 'is' and what 'should be'.

Tension in time and space

The dimensions of time and space are always present in any issue. In your mind, things should happen at the right time and place and would cause tension if it's not the case.

And relax....

When you can consider what 'is' and what 'should be' objectively, you are less frustrated. Once you realise the tension doesn't serve you, you are able to release the pressure.

Balance

In contrast to everyday life, a holiday is self-contained, time-limited, and outside the environment that causes pressure. You can enjoy yourself relaxing and releasing tension, stress-free, even if it is an active holiday. As such, there are benefits to taking time off.

Acceptance

People know they are tense. They know they should relax and release the tension to move on, but they are in a paradox. Relaxing becomes a domination, something they should do, and therefore they react and rebel against telling themselves they should relax.

The gearbox model

When faced with a task that you need to do, you are better off without the pressure. It is like when an engine begins to labour, you would change gear. In your case, acknowledge that you have the pressure, accept that it doesn't help, agree it would be better without, and decide what you want to do. Once you have decided, tension dissipates.

An important detail

When the demands of the situation makes you anxious, you can be reassured by saying positive things to yourself. As a result, you increase your resources and are less overwhelmed.

Habituation

It is about learning to progressively remain in a good state whilst considering something that normally makes you react.

Becoming creative

When you are free of tension, you are free of automatic responses and can create rather than react. Otherwise, by default, the mind will not be able to escape the pull of the tension in a situation.

Stuck and can't move on

Nature abhors a vacuum. When you miss someone or something, you keep reminiscing about what you miss. Your mind flip flops between something or someone that was once there, and its absence. Lamenting this loss has more to do with filling a vacuum than love.

Outside of your control

It is crucial to deal with only what is in your control. Otherwise, you trap yourself in a problem that you can't resolve. But you can work on your control.

Boundaries

We react when someone trespasses the boundaries of our values. To be in control, we need boundaries and putting limits on what is acceptable or not.

Relationships

In working relationships, we keep clear boundaries, but in a romantic relationship, we test boundaries to check the relationship is safe. The partners in a relationship are playing a game. It is important to figure out the rules of the game.

Projections

We project characteristics, traits, qualities, or intentions on people. We are doing it all the time. Especially with the people that matter to us, including our families and significant others.

Games

In a relationship, partners react to whatever is happening in relation to what should be happening. It makes them frustrated, angry, disappointed, or surprised and happy. What ensues is a predictable set of moves and reactions: a game.

Contracting

Contracting is not only with others, you also contract with yourself. Unless you make explicit what you are going to do and what you would get from it. i.e. the terms of the contract, things are unpredictable and can go wrong.

The game of procrastination

Becoming aware of your pattern of avoidance may not stop your procrastinating, but observing it will start to ease a change.

Good habits and attitudes

On breathing

You can regain control of what is happening by establishing control of your breathing.

Meditation

The point of meditation is being aware of your thoughts happening without getting carried away. This ability is equally helpful in real life.

Trance and awareness

Trance bypasses the censorship that a stressed mind would impose on thinking.

Trance is a rehearsal. When you rehearse, you come close to the real thing.

Planning a future

It is difficult to think of the future when unhappy about the past and frustrated about the present. When you plan, you create a future, giving you something to look forward to, a sense of direction.

About intentions
Intentions need nurturing and time.

Purpose
This chapter is about the ongoing feedback you get when what you are doing is on purpose.

Emergent quality
When we want to fulfil a purpose, problems arise as we are caught in cause and effect. When we try to cause something as a means to an end, we tense because our expectations are not always fulfilled and it questions our control. If we focus on creating the right conditions for something to happen, we can let go of controlling what we can't.

Harmony
The mind behaves in the same way as our immune system. What doesn't belong is rejected. Life works when we are in a state of belonging. Doubt and questioning oneself will always be there, but we have the choice of accepting that it belongs in how we operate. That chronic tension is part of who we are.

Surrender
Anger, sadness, and depression exist because of the ego. When you transcend the ego, you can let go of self-centeredness and be in harmony with life.

Existential considerations
At times, we realise life is meaningless, and at other times, creating meaning is compulsive. We can't help it. Which one is it? You can get stuck in meaninglessness or meaningfulness or not be able to decide which way it is.

Develop your best state
When you are in the flow, you are in a state of optimum tension/relaxation for the performance of any task.

Therefore, identifying and practising that state is one of the best things you can do.

Life's demands

Life will throw a spanner in the works despite your best intentions and efforts. Life is what happens when you are busy making plans. Be aware of that, and don't let go of your good work.

Creating a virtuous circle

When you are considering all the suggestions for improving your life, pick something that works for you and notice the difference it makes. Cultivate it. Then you will reverse being in a vicious circle into being in a virtuous circle.

Gratitude

Gratitude is a productive and useful way of generating feedback and create a virtuous circle. It is an acknowledgment of what is and appreciating its value.

What's Next?

Apply what you have learnt and develop your conviction that you are on the way.

"I think the most important question facing humanity is, 'Is the universe a friendly place?' This is the first and most basic question all people must answer for themselves.

For if we decide that the universe is an unfriendly place, then we will use our technology, our scientific discoveries, and our natural resources to achieve safety and power by creating bigger walls to keep out the unfriendliness and bigger weapons to destroy all that which is unfriendly and I believe that we are getting to a place where technology is powerful enough that we may either completely isolate or destroy ourselves as well in this process.

If we decide that the universe is neither friendly nor unfriendly and that God is essentially 'playing dice with the universe,' then we are simply victims to the random toss of the dice and our lives have no real purpose or meaning.

But if we decide that the universe is a friendly place, then we will use our technology, our scientific discoveries, and our natural resources to create tools and models for understanding that universe. Because power and safety will come through understanding its workings and its motives."

"God does not play dice with the universe."

Albert Einstein (Allegedly. Origins uncertain.)

Life is stressful

Our interaction with the world leads to some conclusions; things happen and we interpret them. At the end of the implications, it ultimately boils down to:

"Is the world a friendly place?"

You enter a new environment you have never been in and you wonder: Are these people friendly or not? Do I like them? Do they like me? Can I relax or should I be on guard? If you don't know the person who has knocked on your door, what is your reaction? Similarly, if someone stops you in the street and asks "Can you help me?"

There is always this assessment wherever you are in your life: is it safe, neutral, or dangerous?

It's a subconscious assessment everybody makes when they go somewhere. Even if you think you are confident and at ease in social situations, this programming is always running in the background. In any case, it takes little for it to be activated. We have to be on the lookout, stay alert, and remain wary and attentive.

If you feel that the world is not a friendly place, it can be about a specific situation, as in when you have a bad experience with customer service, or life in general. Do you see those incidents as exceptions, or representative of how the world is? Your attitude to life could be expressed as chronic anger, triggered by what has happened to you in the past. It can be anticipatory of the future, as in anxiety, what could happen? You don't know; better to be guarded; be vigilant. You are now on tenterhooks; on alert. Your attitude to the world, life, permeates your being and mood in all areas of your life, such as how you relate to other people. In fact, it's probably the cornerstone of your life. This perception affects everything. It organises how you perceive what is happening, how you organise the information and what you do with it.

When something happens, do you become defensive or aggressive or simply see it as a problem to solve? Perhaps you are positive and trusting or doubting and cynical. Your attitude to life and the world determines whether you are happy to take risks, get involved, commit, and contribute. It affects how you manage your resources, time and energy, or freely share or protect your ideas,

Each and every one of us is on the continuum: life is a friendly place versus life is unsafe. It's expressed in our temperament, but it also changes throughout life, depending on the circumstances we find ourselves in. Problems will arise, and there will be things to be concerned about. When we go on holiday, suddenly everyone seems nicer. You treat people amicably and everyone seems amicable to you too. The world is suddenly a friendly place. It's an exception from everyday life. The response is usually overcompensating; from a bad place, the world now becomes a great place. For some, it is the opposite: they go abroad and are suspicious of the locals. They are out to get you because you are a tourist!

You are in a bad mood, and that's it. It's all doom and gloom. And the way you look at the world is tainted. Your thinking is more polarised, more black and white. Whatever the circumstances, everyone is wondering about the context of their lives, whether today, the year ahead, or their entire lives. We live in a continuum of relaxation versus stress, depending on how we perceive the world, or life around us, whether it is benevolent, whether it does as we want it to, or not.

Whether you were either nurtured or neglected, your early upbringing will influence your response. For example, if you were loved and cherished, you would believe and find evidence that the universe is a friendly place. But if you had to fend for yourself, you may be guarded and assume challenges and negative consequences.

It particularly seems to be the case for teenagers and young adults. From many parents, I hear that their children have a reactive attitude. They don't want to participate or help in the house. They have a significant existential crisis wishing to be somebody, and the world treating them as if they are nobody. They have high expectations of themselves from social media, films, and TV. They want to be seen by others as being up there with a socially recognised status. A friend of mine has a daughter. She works in a temporary job because she can't find a job in the area she studied. The reality of life is such a let-down for teenagers. It is a terrible blow. They are under the thumb of their parents who have sold out, going into boring jobs and having boring lives. It's embarrassing. The youngsters are stuck in a rut, and their egos can't accept it. So they rebel in the form of a passive-aggressive attitude. From managers, I hear that many carry this attitude into the workplace. Teenagers are more reactive and expressive about it. The rest of the population also experiences dissatisfaction and unfulfilled expectations but are numbed and resigned to accepting their lot.

> At the end of each chapter, I will encourage you to reflect or observe what you are doing. In the first part of the book, the point is not to change anything but for you to become aware of your habits and thoughts. Beware, your eagerness to try to fix something before it can be addressed would exacerbate your stress.

For this first chapter, why don't you start by spending some time thinking about contexts when you feel the world, life, or people are friendly and when they are not?

The point is to realise that this assessment of the world influences everything: your attitude, beliefs, and behaviour.

Stress

Our inability to deal with the world and react to what's happening creates stress.

I did Aikido classes, a martial art. In early lessons, we learnt to deal with someone attacking us with a wooden knife. If it was a real knife, it would be too dangerous. The stress of what could happen if something went wrong (being stabbed) would have prevented us from focusing on learning to move in the right way. But because that threat was taken care of, we could learn and deal appropriately with the object. Until you have built the automatic responses, you cannot go through the same reactions with real knives. (I am still only competent in dealing with wooden knife attacks).

We talk about good stress when we choose to take on a challenge, like in sport, and bad stress when we don't have the resources to address the demands of a situation. It implies not being in control. It implies danger.

Stress affects your state of mind. When you feel you are not in control and stressed, you become anxious and tense. It becomes a vicious circle. You are anxious and therefore become hyper-vigilant about what could go wrong. As a result, you become overwhelmed and consequently feel out of control.

Meerkats, native to South African deserts, always have a few of their party standing straight up, scanning the landscape and the sky for danger. They are tense and alert but regularly swap roles to relax, forage for something to eat, play, and let go of their accumulated stress. Most humans don't regulate their behaviour in this way and are in chronic stress mode.

Very few people are capable of re-focussing on what they have control of when they are stressed. The lack of control can make us tense and reactive. The tension felt in the body makes us interpret what is happening as not having control. It generalises quickly.

As a meaning-making machine, we humans can't help but interpret what is happening outside, around us, and what's happening inside, our feelings and emotions. We don't just get raw data from our senses. Everything you perceive, think, and feel comes with attached interpretation: you feel good, bad, better, worse. When you are exposed to something that stresses you, the combined aspect of the object's meaning and the feeling of stress feeds back into the system in a distorted way.

To remain in control, we must assess the danger. However, when we are stressed about something, we perceive it differently. As a result, we overestimate the amount of risk in the situation, feeding more stress and anxiety into the system. It's a cycle that needs to be broken, both long-term in reaction to that situation, but even short-term. We break away from the situation by stopping for a moment and then applying logic. We can do that by giving ourselves a pause for the adrenaline to go down. We can take some slow deep breaths and do something else to break the pattern, like going for a short walk, or staring at an object and reminiscing about what is associated with it.

We have a compulsion to apply a solution before understanding the problem objectively. It may be appropriate when we need to react quickly, but not when a problem persists. That is why I encourage you to read the first part of the book just to raise your awareness, rather than jumping into solutions.

Unless you are enlightened, or believe you are the creator of your reality, you can't help it. Your experience is the way it is. You are the way you are. It is virtually impossible to discern that you create your reality when stressed. The danger forces you to focus on the external situation. It's a survival instinct, one that takes precedence over anything else. You have no choice in the matter.

The ego has to interpret everything around us, with us at the centre of the universe. We are right; others, the world, and timing are all wrong. You cannot take perspective and be objective. Stress creates a small mind and a narrow focus. You have to concentrate on what the object that scares you does.

Anyone familiar with cats would know that the relaxed kitty is malleable; you can do what you want with it, but there is no way to get anything out of it when it is stressed. We are not so dissimilar. When stressed, the proof is in how we feel.

Think of something that stresses you. Aim at noticing the two aspects: the problem you are facing and the stress. Try to dissociate the two. You don't have to do anything else than being aware of those two aspects.

Resources and demands

When we think of the demands and the resources available in any situation, they appear factual and static. When we think, we take stock and evaluate the risks and benefits, with ideas and facts that are fixed.

In reality, everything is in a constant state of fluctuation. When the demand increases, the resources are affected. When the resources increase, the demand doesn't affect us as much.

Here is a personal example. In July 2019, I went to the French Alps and walked the steep paths to the top of one of the majestic peaks. Those paths that sometimes appear from afar, like a scratch line on the side of the mountain. A line that people travel on, like ants, but much slower. When going up, I was breathing heavily due to my low fitness level. However, I was not overly concerned. I thought this was as it should be. I was at the limit of being able to cope with the task, but it was sustainable. I avoided adding the stress of my mind to the stress on my body. Normally we start to stress about what will happen and worry, but I kept in control, so I continued steadily. The descent was not a strenuous effort any more. However, the strain on the muscles and joints was different. My right knee started to hurt. It soon became unbearable and I was limping. I could not comfortably do one step after the other.

You see it with older people who are very cautious because they cannot quickly re-establish their balance. The consequence of losing balance is to fall, and if they fall, that would be catastrophic, resulting in them hurting themselves very badly. Their ability to deal with the unexpected becomes reduced. The capacity to manage the next step is not the same as when they were younger. Then, they knew they could manage the descent. It was an exciting challenge where they quickly found their footing again if they had momentarily lost it. They could deal with whatever comes up. Climbing the mountain was fun.

Back to my descent, it was a long ongoing effort, where each step accomplished was a relief and the next one a risky, stressful demand. The unrelenting demand was tiring. I now questioned the presumption I had about being able to walk this challenging path. I was struggling to cope with the situation. I became aware of time as if I was in a competition and needed to finish in a given time. Like the space, time was against me. The remote possibility of something bad happening became more likely. So much so that the risk became increasingly probable. It could happen.

The pain made me constantly scan for danger, as in the risk of my weakened wobbly right leg not being able to support my body. The narrow, slippery path was covered with small loose stones carved on a steep rock face. If I were to slip, I would have nothing to grab on to and crash to the bottom of the mountain. "Woah, stop looking to the side. It makes you dizzy". "You have to focus on the next step ahead of you." This repeated pattern of being pulled by the void and focusing on the painful next step made the rest of the descent exhausting.

In this example, I refer to my resources as my ability to walk, sustain the effort, know where to put my foot, quickly re-establish my balance if I slip on little rocks, and stop. I can do all that. I refer to the demands as the effort required to follow others at their pace, the need to be vigilant of dangers, and the heat: it was the middle of the summer. Those are the constraints of the situation. The demands increased as my resources, the ability to walk confidently and competently, diminished.

Did I feel the need for a lullaby when I went to bed? Oh no, I was knackered!

Everyone experiences a similar personal version of my descent. Their own version of being overwhelmed by the demands. Then they become reactive, aggressive, and depressed.

Transactional Analysis, a psychodynamic psychotherapy (a form of psychology that derives from Freudian principles of subconscious motivation stemming from early experiences), describes our way of responding to the pressure of demands, known as drivers. They are rules that guide our life. It shapes our personalities. We get them from the important people in our childhood.

The drivers are "Be Perfect," "Be Strong," "Hurry Up," "Try Hard," and "Please Me." Those are the commands we give ourselves when we are stressed. They are supposed to spur us into a way of dealing with the demand as it should be. For example, if I am under pressure, I should respond by being strong. Unfortunately, it makes us respond rigidly and dogmatically, which exacerbates rather than solves the situation. It increases our tension rather than giving us flexibility. It is useful to be aware of the drivers that control you and explain your personality or that of others.

"Be Perfect": when stressed, you focus on details. It's never good enough.

"Be Strong": don't be weak and get on with it. Blame others if they are weak.

"Hurry Up": the pressure makes you want to do things quickly; you are impatient with yourself and others.

"Try Hard": don't give up. Be determined.

"Please Me": You become a placater, constantly checking if others are happy. You do what they want and ignore your own needs.

It is also what we want other people to be. So another's behaviour usually exacerbates ours, and we emphasise our drivers. For example, becoming a tyrant when we feel people are weak or becoming very sensitive to the moods of others when we are stressed.

At work, it may be you're struggling with saying no when asked to do something by a manager, like working at the weekend or staying longer hours. You may have a driver which does not authorise you to say "no". You may not have dared to say no to your father. Those rules that you have swallowed whole may be toxic. It may help some readers to know some of these negative drivers are external and symptomatic of negative or archaic opinions, especially in a working environment where there is much stress.

Awareness of our habits is the beginning of changing them.

Awareness helps us to have more compassion for ourselves and others. Tension and inflexibility lead to suffering. Compassion softens that tension and thus leads to acceptance. For example, in the context of depression, some may blame themselves because it is a sign of weakness. However, it might not be the case if you did not have a driver to be strong.

It is not just humans that experience stress. The whole living world does. Stress creates tension, which is used in the fight, flight, and freeze response. The zebra senses the lion and keeps a safe distance to stay in control. If it is surprised, it would use more tension and dash and run fast. Otherwise, it would trot or walk away. Just the right amount not to respond unnecessarily and therefore be depleted of its energy. It manages its stress and tension. In fact, in herds, one member would usually get closer to the danger to see better what is going on so that others can react appropriately if need be. Millions of people worldwide struggle to cope with the relentless demands placed on them. Unlike the zebra, they can't walk away from their source of stress and are constantly under pressure.

Everyone I meet in the public or private sector complains about having to do more with less. Even children are on a punitive scholastic schedule with overwhelming expectations.

Day after day, the demands grind people down. Sleeping is not enough. They are so tired they can't even sleep properly. Not relaxed enough to undo the tension, they burn out. They go into manic depression, become hyperactive, and go into overdrive, followed by bouts of depression because they cannot cope. It's no wonder zombie movies are popular. At least we are less worse off than them. It's reassuring.

The description of not having the resources to deal with the demand is analysed throughout this book by looking at various aspects and taking different perspectives to look at the same thing. Hopefully, this book should give you an awareness of your behaviour and more control, or at least give you the benefit of understanding that it is not your fault that you can't cope in certain situations or life in general.

We are going to look at resources and demand. Take a specific aspect of your life. I will take cooking. Your resources are your knowledge of the principles of cooking and preparing food, the ingredients you have, a recipe book, time, and kitchen utensils. The demands are your expectations about the result or those of people who come for dinner; time, as in deadline; paying attention to several things happening at once, i.e., don't let the potatoes overcook whilst you slice the onions. All those elements are static.

Now imagine a guest comes early; it affects the demand. You were fine with your original plan. Demands and resources were balanced. Now you have to divide your attention. See how it puts a strain on your resources? You realise you forgot to buy the main ingredient, and now you are under pressure to change your plan. It is the dynamic aspect of the variability of resources and demands.

Pick an activity and think about how you would plan it.

Notice how what you planned can be thrown out by reality and how it would affect the balance of resources and demands.

Take a few minutes to refocus and rethink the task.

Domination

The unwanted demands of a situation make you feel dominated as you feel forced to do or experience something you don't want to do. People are often not aware of it happening, whether it is imposed by others, themselves, or a combination of the two.

Whether they go to see a therapist or go on a date, some people are guarded. They partially initiate the situation, such as making an appointment, but also partially resist being in it. Even in established love relationships, the partners may not be totally open. They keep some cards close to their chest, whether it is to protect the other, the relationship, or themselves; better to be safe than sorry. Otherwise, it will be another example of being dominated by whatever could come up. It's the opposite of a child's nature, which is free, direct, and self-expressed about their needs and feelings. Letting oneself be vulnerable is surrendering rather than reacting to the domination of a situation.

A client of mine said, "If there is external pressure, I don't like it. I don't like people telling me what to do. I don't want to lose control."

We all want to be free of any authority until subservience is beaten into us by fear and punishment. Then, what we see outside is replicated internally. One becomes a slave to the ideas and beliefs that we have created.

We all have tasks that we avoid, be it the tax return, the difficult communication you have to deliver, or the spring cleaning of your wardrobe. So take something you put off and check: do you feel oppressed by it?

Have you ever heard a 'ping' sound that informs you that an email has arrived? You are annoyed. Having to deal with it is imposed on you. You subsequently feel dominated by it.

Even the activities we enjoy doing sometimes becomes a chore. It becomes an imposition. How many books have been bought and stay on the bedside tables? They become evidence of a to-do—another domination.

We tell ourselves not to have dessert if we want to lose weight or not to have a beer or a glass of wine, and we moan. We feel dominated by this self-inflicted command. We end up negotiating an exception.

It starts very early in life when a toddler doesn't want to stay in his pushchair. He will feel oppressed and do all he can to avoid being dominated by his parent. His reaction is to throw a tantrum and get angry. It is less intense when he is a teenager but more chronic. Always whining or feeling overwhelmed. Having to go to school, wake up early, clean his room, abide by parents or society's rules... argh.... Total domination. "I am not your slave."

Even babies: I observed a mum trying to spoon-feed a baby. He refused to eat, and the more he reacted against the domination of being fed, the more he was active with his hands, trying to reach and shake anything in proximity, compensating for being dominated by the spoon that fed him by being very active. So lack of control in one area switched to controlling whatever he could.

That feeling of being dominated is chronic. The weight of should do" is heavy. Any parental or authority figure's request is reacted against.

But not only from other people. Most of our avoidance of what we perceive as domination comes from ourselves. That terrible beginning of the year when we decided that we would join a gym, be healthier, lose weight, put time aside to read those books we always wanted to read, do some voluntary work, be more social, and host dinners. Sooner or later, they become a bore and a chore. We curse the time we made the commitment. "Why did I say I was going to that thing?". We may not have started at all or have started and found it too much. It dominates us. Many people sign for courses, pay and don't turn up. You often read the ten tips to make your resolutions work in magazines, but ultimately, those are still ways to reduce or bypass the domination of those ill-conceived resolutions. Those tips add to the burden!

What I feel dominated by is entirely different from my peers, and they may find it hard to understand why I might feel such a way towards something so mundane and straightforward. The solutions they propose do not consider my context, concerns, fears, capability, and what has to happen before something else happens.

Several of my male friends would not go to a doctor. They may have pain or disturbing symptoms, but they would not go. It may be a mix of a "be strong" driver and avoiding the domination of whatever is there for them. They would not want to talk about it anyway. Questioning them would be experienced as domination.

Think of something you thought was a good idea, like a diet you were going to follow or an exercise you were going to do.

Experience the domination of what you should be doing and notice your urge to escape. Stay with it. Is it a heavy feeling, a pressure, a darkening of your vision? Explore it.

Additionally, you can list those things you should do, but you don't.

Where do they come from?

How did they become dominations?

For instance, a psychological driver to lose weight or be more social. Perhaps pressures come from a society that we feel we must conform to in order to be accepted or happy?

Part of understanding triggers can be an acceptance of such things.

Hopelessness and control

When you are overwhelmed or dominated, you can't cope. It often triggers and relates to other examples of not being able to cope in the past. You don't have to look for them; they present themselves. You were not in control of your life in the past. You are not now. It implies you won't be in the future either. It extends forward. The feeling of hopelessness drives what you are finding and reinforces it. You feel hopeless, and the evidence effortlessly presents itself. You can't even control your lack of control. It controls you.

You usually focus on what is missing. There is always some information you don't have or aspects you can't predict. So there is reinforcement that you are not in control. Then you blame yourself for putting yourself in this bad situation, leading to ulcers or depression. You did wrong, and you punish yourself.

This explains why people are stuck in a morass of depression. The most practised activity is thinking depressing thoughts. Even if something good happens, it sinks into the quicksand of despair. Hopelessness brings you back to the normal state of affairs: gloominess, apathy, discomfort. Avoidance becomes the prime focus of attention. It is like a safety-conscious parent ensuring that you don't wander out in the wilderness where you don't belong, where it is unsafe. Depression and frustration may be unpleasant, but it is familiar and safe. It is bad, but at least it doesn't get any worse.

Have you ever been hesitant or refused to do something when someone gave you instructions? Of course, the implications of something going wrong matter. For example, you might hesitate if someone were to invite you to operate heavy machinery, even if he said he would tell you what to do. It is something you may have seen in movies, where the pilot is out of action, and someone else has to land the plane. They are never enthusiastic about it!

There is another aspect. When someone briefs us on what we don't know, they focus on what we should know. However, we are concerned about what else could come up. There are things we should know, but what we fear is what we don't know, which is the background information that the person who briefs you takes for granted. For example, if someone asks you to cover reception, they would talk you through how to do it. You make sure you know the procedures, but what concerns you is everything else that could happen that they haven't told you. The 'what if's. What if a visitor asks you something you don't know? What if something happens and you don't know how to handle it?

Have you noticed when you read instructions manuals, for e.g. a computer, help pages always give instructions for common issues but quite often, the instructions seldom seem to fit your situation? "Pull down the menu, go to settings, advanced settings, and press the box saying "press this box." Yet, there never seems to be a box or the option they are describing. As a result, we become frustrated, setting us up to avoid the situation. People fear that they won't be able to deal with the situation or that something bad will happen, so they don't engage in the first place.

Pick an activity that you would not take part in, like addressing a crowd or jumping off an airplane. What would be your justification for not doing it?

Those are probably activities you can avoid. What about those you can't? You have to do things you don't like but have no choice but to do. Experience the domination of that.

How do you deal with not having control?

Passivity and belonging

The concept of whether the world is a safe place and how it treats us is connected to whether we feel like we belong. I started the book on the premise "Is the world a friendly place?" as the most basic conclusion we come to about life, but I could have as easily had its closest relative: "Do I belong?" Belonging or not belonging is a fundamental position in the world. It operates at a mundane, practical level as well as at a spiritual, existential level. It is a state of being in a familiar space and time, like your office on Monday or with your family for Sunday lunch. It's the default setting. It organises and leads to everything being possible or probable, or impossible or improbable. If you are amongst your friends, expressing yourself is natural because you belong. However, everything you normally take for granted is under question if you are on the other side of the world, in a new group of people, or in a new context where you don't belong. And you are probably filled with angst. You don't know if what people are saying is serious; is it literal? Are they joking? And unconsciously, you would wonder what the implications are.

I will start with a story. Mary was amongst colleagues who planned to go out after work for a social drink. They discussed it in her presence, but no one invited her. Although she couldn't go because she had a previous engagement anyway, she felt very sad when they did not include her. It triggered her fear of exclusion, which is quite natural. She was angry about their behaviour and felt sorry for herself. I encouraged her to ask them why they had not asked her. She did and found that there was indeed a reason.

However valid it was, their reason did not quench her feeling of not belonging and being isolated. Historically, she'd had many instances when this had happened to her. She also felt that it was about her inability to express herself. The incident, even when resolved, was an example of this issue.

When we don't feel we belong because we have been excluded, we are usually passive, like a powerless child. Something happens to us. We are a victim. We want to be rescued or disappear in escapism, like going for a walk, eating sweet things, or drinking. It's a form of trance being in another reality, detached from here and now. To escape is the way to be active.

You can be active in order to belong. For example, asking the other person how they are, or introducing yourself in relation to the context. What can you do to belong to what you feel excluded from, including life?

You may have instances in the past where you have done that: You paid compliments, asked questions, joined in the activity, or shared an anecdote. You made yourself belong. And in turn, the others thought you belonged. When you initiate a response, you get one.

Belonging is an active process. Mary had choice and control. Being in victim mode is passive. Being free and belonging is active. It's not about what is happening but about what you make happen. Your concept of self may include finding out about people when you don't know them, asking them questions, and being interested.

I once helped a client resolve his fear of water solely by reflecting on belonging in the swimming pool, the shallow end, as well as the deep end.

Remember, this part of the book is still about becoming aware, not about tips on how to...

Take a context where you belong; it can literally be a place where you have friends or you are familiar with. For example, you go to a party. Your friends will be there. They will be happy to see you. Even an annoying individual will be there. The people, what they do or say are part of that context. Notice how every part belongs to the context, even you.

Now take something that you would find embarrassing or that you find scary. Consider that you don't belong to that context. What it is in those contexts that makes you not belong?

Notice your reaction when you are in a context where you belong, and when you are in a context when you don't belong. Notice in both your being active and being passive.

Tension and reaction

There are always aspects that you can control and others that you can't, but when you are stressed, you cannot distinguish that. If you could make the distinction, you would not be tense or reactive. Instead, you would feel detached, objective, and in control.

When you are in control, it is different because you choose the context in which to be tense. For example, you may enjoy the intense emotions of watching a horror movie. Another example is seeing the supporters of a football team going through all the emotions caused by what is happening on the pitch. Normally composed men and women are in all states when their team scores or hold their heads in disbelief when they lose. A lot of tension is accumulated and suddenly released. They can enjoy the trepidations, the ups and downs of what is happening on the pitch, because they have chosen the context and therefore are in control.

The build-up of tension and its release is also why we want to find a sexual partner or how magic and humour work.

Think of a spring: when compressed, it is ready to spring back. Our body and mind are the same. The more stressed you are, the more tense you are, and the more reactive you are. It is probably one of the most important messages of this book. Tension leads to being reactive.

The dynamic of thinking, feeling, and doing is the crux. We usually put our attention on thinking because we need to justify why we feel bad. We ruminate on the thoughts and scenarios and continue to speculate.

When something bad, frustrating, or scary happens, do we resolve it calmly, logically, or factually?

No. Instead, we gossip about it to ourselves, friends, and family. What transpires is a monologue or discussion about reasons and causes which feeds the anxiety. Causation and consequences become blurred. We don't know which one is which. Because the mind is geared towards making connections and links, there is plenty of evidence and matter to discuss.

A mother reported that she had a heated argument with her son. Because he was going on a gap year abroad, he had brought all his stuff to her flat. She was not happy about it and wanted him to remove his things from her living room before he left on his trip. The argument started. The boy felt he had no choice. He did not know where else to put his belongings. It was his only option. He felt trapped, and he became tense and fearful and responded aggressively. What was happening to the boy was also happening to the mother. She also felt like she was placed in a situation with no way out. She became fearful and tense. She felt trapped; he felt trapped. It could only escalate into an argument or a fight.

Often though, we want and create tension and stress. In good stress, like in physical activities, the tension in the muscle is required to react to the demand. For example, a tennis player needs tension in his body to hit the ball, to react at the right moment, in the right way. It is natural.

In the office, having to pick up the phone to talk to someone to make a request would cause tension, because we don't know how they are going to respond.

When we try to figure out something, not knowing creates tension. There is a pressure of having to figure it out. it dominates what you have to accomplish. But knowing releases tension and eases the flow.

Good ideas emerge from a creative state. That moment of "Ah ha" recognition when the piece fits in the map, and affects your understanding of the whole picture releases tension.

In yoga, you intentionally create tension by stretching, you also need to relax at the same time. After a match, the sportsman can relax, but he needs to have the right amount of tension during the match. By balancing tension and relaxation simultaneously, he responds to the situation's demand, but he is not overwhelmed or trying to avoid the demand. In other words, he is in control. That is what happens when a person is in the flow. It can happen in sports, and it can happen in other aspects of life. There needs to be a good balance between tension and relaxation to respond optimally to the demands of the situation.

We can release tension naturally or deliberately during and after the effort, but we may also not want to release it because it's our personality: Hard work is good. The tension is a good reminder of what we have achieved, like muscle pain after a good workout. However, when people are overly stressed, they tense up and become reactive. They can't relax any more. When it happens, the thinking becomes either/or, black or white, yes or no. You are either in control, or you're not. You feel dominated, pressured by the demand, and not in control. You are like a ball in a pinball machine, pushed and pulled by the demands of life. And you don't like it.

How do you know that you can trust the other person? People would know most of the time because they don't perceive tension in the other person. If they do, they will tense too. First, they sense and then look for a rational explanation to justify their feelings. Tension communicates to oneself and others. People, and women, in particular, are very sensitive to others being tense, especially when they have their antennas out to scan for incongruence. Incongruence would be sensed as tension. That tension may come from the fear of being judged. And there you have a vicious circle. One checks for signs of tension, and the other tenses because they are being checked.

Animals who live in groups are very sensitive to each other's signals. Impalas, zebras, and wildebeests gather together to have as many eyes and ears open to potential predators. What communicates is tension. Tension and nervousness imply danger. The lack of it means that everything is fine. The same happens to us collectively, in-crowd phenomena, but also intrinsically. We tense, we feel fearful and anxious, meaning there must be danger. We are more sensitive to loss than we are to gain. So until we get the all-clear, we should stay tense, alert, and ready to act.

Verify for yourself how tension communicates.

Tense voluntarily.

Tighten your muscles, clench your jaws, frown.

Notice how you feel.

Do you have a sense that something will happen and that you have to be ready?

Notice how tension changed your attitude.

Deciding

Throughout life, we have to make decisions. The process produces tension, as there is a possible risk of making the wrong choice. If you decide this, you won't have that. If you decide to stay at home instead of going out, all the possibilities that could have happened if you had gone out will not happen. What if it is the wrong choice? The perceived loss creates tension. It isn't easy to let go. It is sometimes described as the fear of missing out.

The decision process is stressful, but even if you postpone deciding to relieve the tension of missing out, it would still be stressful because you know you cannot make decisions.

Deciding works at several intertwined levels:

1. The content, the implications of your choice, the consequences.

2. Your capability in deciding the matter at hand, how you prioritise or organise, and your confidence in making decisions. You may not know about the subject matter, but you know you have the skills to make decisions across different contexts.

3. Your identity, the kind of person you are, and who is in control or not in control.

4. The growing tension associated with not yet deciding. When the pressure hits a threshold, you would have to decide, and postponing comes at a cost.

It affects your present and your future. You can't project yourself in the future if you are not confident. You also find all the evidence that you were unable to make decisions in the past. Or maybe not: in the past, you could decide! So now it is even worse because the comparison between now, (being stuck), and then, (when you could), means it is getting worse.

Deciding can also be liberating; you feel better once you have decided. It releases tension as long as, based on a rational comparison of pros and cons, you are complete with your choice.

If you experience deciding as being aware that the implications of the two options are ultimately unknowable, you would release the tension. Would the other side be greener? You may never know but would feel good about having decided.

Feeling that you are not in control makes deciding difficult. But in turn, being able to decide generates energy and makes you feel more in control, able to decide what you need to do.

One way to develop your decision making, and therefore increasing your control, is to pay attention to the fact that whatever you do comes out of a decision. You may not have been aware that you made a decision, but you did: you move your position as you read this book, because you have been in the same position for too long. If you can spot yourself doing it and attributing it to a decision you made, it is progress. Even the most trivial things, like you had an itch and you scratch, derives from a decision.

If you can notice that everything you do is out of a decision, you start to regain control and consequently generate energy that allows you to make bigger decisions.

To decide between options that matter to you, you may have to wait for the tension to release. Maybe you have a decision you know you have to make right now.

How would the decision be easier to make if you could let go of the tension?

Try, what would it be like if you didn't have that pressure? What would you decide?

Prediction

Not knowing what is going to happen next means you are on a slippery slope that you can't control. The feeling is one you want to avoid at all costs. When you have to do something or are being asked to do something, and you don't know what will happen, it is like being on a slide that becomes increasingly steep and where you don't know where you are going to land. It provokes an increasing physical revulsion. It is terrifying. There is a ripple of consequences that you don't control, and it viscerally grips you. It's as if someone wants to push you in the swimming pool and you don't know how to swim. They push and you resist and increasingly start to panic.

All of this is in the context of you not knowing what will happen, meaning you are not in control. If you had done it before, you would be in control. You may not know some aspects, but you know you can improvise. It's like playing. There are elements known, others unknown. You know your friend hides, but you don't know where. You know how to seek. You would be in control as you choose to engage in the activity. Some people are quite happy to take on whatever comes their way, going somewhere they have never been, doing something they have never done, or interacting with people they have never met. Others are very cautious of the unknown. Their usual initial reaction is "I don't know how to" or "But you don't know how to". The former think in terms of what, the latter in terms of how. Those who think in terms of what consider what is to be done, and why, and they are not concerned about how. They know they will figure it out in good time, as it comes. Whereas the people who tend to think in terms of how are reluctant to deal with anything new. It is their first reaction: "I don't know…" Except if they have managed to build themselves a very predictable and secure routine, life is always knocking at the door with unpredictable events, and it is a source of anxiety. They are prone to react negatively to unsolicited demands. Unless there is a very clear detailed breakdown of what needs to be done, they won't do the task. I can think of people who choose not to have a smartphone, because they don't know how to use one, or not go abroad if people don't speak English at their destination, or prefer not to engage in a social activity because they don't know how they are supposed to behave.

As a child, when you have to say hello to a stranger, it is unfamiliar; therefore, you are apprehensive. For the parent, saying hello to a stranger is known and risk-free; they are familiar with it. Perhaps your fear could be having to fill out a form, and you don't know how to answer; you get a gut reaction that you want to avoid. You are conflicted. You

Regain control of your life

have to, but you can't do it. No wonder you find yourself engaging with something else to distract you. That path is far too distressing: anything but that gut-wrenching physical feeling of being dominated. It makes sense that you'd want to avoid that feeling and replace it with something less unpleasant.

A client of mine said, "I could imagine but don't want it to be true. If true, it would mean I become attached, dependent, no control, no complete control, at the mercy of other people. I don't know."

The whole process of life, even for simple lifeforms, is to predict the interaction with the environment. By that, I mean other people, events, life, to know if it is good or bad, friendly or hostile. That is what an amoeba does. That is what a human being does: the same process, at a different level of complexity. As a living entity, we spend our entire lives doing an apprenticeship of that discerning process of what works and what doesn't. We seek more pleasure or avoid more pain. We have discovered recently that even plants do it. They communicate as a network to change their chemical resistance to prepare for an unwanted attack from a parasite, for example clover and caterpillars. It is common to many species.

To predict, we need some certainty. Is it safe or unsafe, friendly or malicious? Can we know? Is it not too complex or complicated? Can we figure it out? Throughout our life, we have experiences from which we understand and learn. When we can't count on ourselves to make decisions, we can't predict. When we can't predict, it creates chronic angst. And when we are not in control of how we can deal with the demand, we feel dominated. It's an all-recursive cause and effect.

Take something you fear doing, like filling out a form where you are asked to supply information you don't have. It could be physical activity, doing DIY, or being invited to dance. It could be answering personal questions or being asked to volunteer in front of an audience.

Notice the feeling of dread as you think you have to do it.

Notice that your mind presents "I don't know how to...", "I don't know what will happen...".

Notice how important it is for you to be able to predict in order to remain in control.

Integrity

When asking the employees of an organisation if what they do has anything to do with the organisation's mission statement, like "We care about our customers," you get instant feedback about the frame of mind of the staff. Either the statement is validated, there is energy, and the staff are happy, or there is no correlation, and you would witness resentment, frustration, or apathy. The same goes for an individual and their own alignment, whether they are following their principles or going in the direction they have decided. The individual will be energised or demotivated.

Integrity, as defined by the dictionary, is the quality or condition of being whole or undivided; completeness. Every action you do has an implicit meaning. If you are not addressing what you know you should do and instead engage in distraction, it communicates something to yourself. It communicates that you are avoiding responsibility and avoiding life. It implies having an issue with your integrity, reliability, and trusting yourself. Either you do what you are supposed to do and feel good, or you don't and you feel bad. That's the simplest denominator. If you don't, you are drained of energy. You feel bad about yourself and therefore need to engage even more in the distracting activity that makes you feel good. People who procrastinate chronically have symptoms similar to depression.

You can't get what you want because it's not clear. You may also feel frustrated that you feel you won't get what you want to start with. Consequently, a feeling of powerlessness is running the show.

When you trust yourself, when you are clear about your situation, where you are going, and your boundaries, you can attend to another person. Otherwise, the other person will sense you're concerned, distracted, or not present.

When you trust yourself, you can trust them. If something they do or say does not suit you, you would just dismiss it, without a fuss, without feeling threatened. If you are unsure that you can trust yourself, you don't trust others.

We don't trust ourselves because, despite good intentions, we don't follow our own lead. We don't follow our lead because we are anxious. It makes where we are going unclear. We don't know why we are going there. We don't know what will happen when we get there. What if something happens that we can't cope with? Anxiety prevents us from focusing on what we may want.

A documentary about the Canadian wilderness depicted a brown bear by a salmon-filled river. It was hungry but anxious because it could smell a grizzly bear nearby. It could not focus on what it wanted: fish. The bear acted as if it was concerned about something that might happen. Its concerns were concrete and immediate.; they were real. The grizzly would not tolerate a competitor. Whereas we, human beings, may have justified threats, but we can also spook ourselves with made-up scenarios we carry around.

Now you think that you can't count on yourself. You don't do what you say you would do. You are unreliable. The relationship with yourself suffers the same as it would if someone else did that to you. Your integrity is worth little. And, of course, like a boat or vessel lacking integrity, you can't rely on it to take you where you want to go.

You have to make do with your unreliable self that you can't count on. You already know that you will not do what you say you are going to do. And therefore, you have even fewer resources to deal with the demand. It affects how you think about the future, what is possible, and what you can decide. Better not take any risk in case of disappointment. It is like a judgement that has been rendered to you. You are punished because you are not good.

You still have to keep yourself occupied.

Reflect on your integrity. Are you doing what you say you are going to do?

Look at your intentions for all areas of your life and what is happening.

See what impact it has.

Notice if it affects your energy, your ability to plan, and your outlook on life.

Final point: this is not an exercise to make you feel bad. Otherwise, you will put this book aside and go and engage in an activity to feel good. Instead, look at it in terms of understanding how you operate. It is necessary before making changes.

Regain control of your life

The behaviours we engage in to avoid anxiety

When we engage in a habitual activity instead of dealing with a task, we do it to feel good. When we feel good, we are able to do things. When we feel bad, we can't. It became clear for a client that her playing Solitaire on her computer was to steady her state. When she anticipated an activity to be challenging, she would feel a bit of anxiety and would instead seek comfort by playing the game.

It is important to have the ability to control our state. Most activities are to steady our state, such as drinking, eating, running, or watching TV. It can be that you need to be calmer, but it could also be that you need to increase your energy. For example, as a child, I witnessed my grandmother moan about a given topic and then give a look of satisfaction because she achieved what she wanted, which was being energised.

Temple Grandin, an American consultant in the cattle industry, happens to be autistic, which gives her an insight into the behaviour and perception of animals. Subsequently, her guidance changed the way cattle is processed in slaughterhouses. One of the things she designed was equipment that would squeeze the cow, which reduces its stress. I had experienced the same thing with a dog. Pluto, my friend's dog, was barking because he reacted to what he could not see properly because of his poor eyesight. We could not stop him by telling him to quiet down. So I grabbed him, hugged him tightly, and he gradually relaxed in my arms. His angry and fearful emotions melted away in the embrace.

There are many examples of strange behaviours people engage in to calm their state. For instance, Jon Richardson, a comedian on the programme "Would I Lie To You" described taking water-free baths to do just that.

Life is stressful, and people seek comfort by avoiding reality. The activities they engage in to cope are not designed to remove the source of the stress but the bad feeling of the stress. They want relief—whatever the means. For example, people in pain take pills to remove pain without addressing the cause. Once the pain disappears, so does their intention. People do the same with life's difficulties and problems.

Distraction from anxiety is not just something that takes your attention away momentarily, like a beautiful butterfly crossing your path. Distraction can be for a moment or last your lifetime. You can live a happy and fulfilled life by creating a 'distraction,' creating your own philosophy, doing things you enjoy, paying attention and appreciating the beauty of life, and being surrounded by people you like including yourself. People find activities to keep occupied. Goals and projects can be considered distractions from the angst of being directionless and purposeless. Better have an occupation, being occupied, than being preoccupied.

Some of those activities are useful or socially approved, such as staying long hours in the office, volunteering, having hobbies or sports, being funny, or adopting a philosophy or a religion. Those activities are not considered negative. Yet, often they are still trying to avoid and prevent something else; loneliness, boredom, angst, or confrontation. They are coping mechanisms. Some are disapproved of, socially looked down upon.

When somebody drinks or eats too much cake; they are subsequently left with the feeling of not doing something they are supposed to do, which is being healthy. They feel they are lacking leadership or direction. Likewise, when a person retires or loses their job, they are sometimes left with a nauseous vacuum; no raison d'être, no direction, no hope.

One of the natural sources of creativity against anxiety is boredom. But, increasingly, talking to other therapists and teachers, it becomes evident that children and teenagers are not utilising their boredom in a creative way. Boredom is naturally a good motivator to be creative and spurs us on to do something. Some parents fill their kids from morning to bedtime with activities for the 16 hours they are awake. Boredom can also be thwarted by social media, TV shows, or computer games that are readily available and endless.

The danger is that children and not only children become passive. They need to be externally stimulated. Otherwise, they fall into a depressive apathy. Unfortunately, they are addicted to external stimulation. I have seen many students who cannot adapt to university because they are required to be self-motivated. They need to quickly relearn intention, attention, feedback, and interest. They need to learn how to respond to passivity and boredom proactively.

We are so used to having our time filled with activities that we don't contemplate our life without them. Consider the quality of your life if you did not have all the activities that filled your time. How would that vacuum feel if you didn't have your job, partner, friends, or habits?

Having a 'to-do'

We are constantly stimulated, and we are so addicted to stimulation that most of us could not do without television or a smartphone. Silence scares many of us because of its absence of stimulation. In contrast, we could practise meditation to have silence. In this silence, truths can be heard or seen.

To avoid the stress of being dominated by something we don't want to face or escape, we engage in trivial behaviour that makes us feel good. You may justify it as useful, such as cleaning or rearranging your furniture or checking if anyone has sent you a message. These may be a good way to reduce your stress and do something useful. But like rearranging the deckchairs on the Titanic, whilst this something to-do gives a feeling of doing something useful, you would not be facing the main thing you have to deal with, whether the issue is important or urgent. The solution becomes a bigger problem, a chronic one. The urgent becomes more urgent; the important becomes more important. So, you face in the other direction, and you don't see it any more. This is what we do as a collective species, we continue contributing to the destruction of our environment, but we find respite in consumerism. The planet's skin is getting ravaged, but we put creams on our own skin because we are worth it. Our cousins, the monkeys, do the same thing: when they are stressed by a tyrannical dominant male, they engage in grooming each other or sex. It is an escape from stress; it feels good and reassuring. We know that the planet is in dire straits, so let's not focus on that. Someone else is going to deal with it. The problem seems too overwhelming, and the possibility of removing the tension is so distant. Instead, let's watch Game of Thrones or read about the relationship between William and Harry or Kate and Meghan!

Regularly, your stressors return to your attention. You still have to deliver that difficult communication, do your tax return or do the spring cleaning of your wardrobe. There is now more urgency as the deadline has arrived. A stressed state leads to a reactive, short-sighted need to relieve the tension. That is where the bad habits are formed, where addictions get reinforced, and a vicious circle is established because there is more urgency to relieve the tension by quickly engaging in a feel-good behaviour. The more urgent the demand of the unwanted obligation, the more urgent the need to escape its domination. The two feed each other. Compulsive behaviour disorder is the extreme form of it.

People can engage in alternative activities and forget what matters. They may be busy with social activities that distract them from their own lives. Yet because they are aware of not doing what they should be doing, it generates anxiety, so they may get even more involved in the activity.

During the Coronavirus isolation, a friend found herself spending most of the day on Facebook. In retrospect, she did not like that she did. She thought it was out of control. To avoid the anxiety of not having the daily routine of going to work, she went on Facebook. That activity offered her a sense of being connected and belonging, the same feelings she got at work. Work gives direction and meaning to life. Trying to do something against spending time on Facebook would be detrimental. I suggested she decides how long she could indulge in that activity. By considering this question, she realised that it would stop naturally when she went back to work. She regained control, and because there was nothing else to do, she perused Facebook without guilt.

This time, examine how it feels to go from the vacuum that you experienced in the previous exercise to the good feeling of having a to-do.

Imagine you have nothing to do and think of something to do.

Notice how it feels. How compulsive and attractive it is.

Not thinking

The good thing about a habitual quick solution is that it doesn't require thinking. It is automatic. When a behaviour is repeated, it becomes a habit. i.e. I don't have to think if I decide to buy a pint of milk. My body knows how to take me to the shop. I give the instruction, "Go get some milk," and I obey. I am on autopilot.

When it is in the context of problem solving, thinking creates tension: the mind tenses, the body tenses. The state of the brain depends on the state of the body. It is the environment in which thinking occurs. When it is in a positive context, problem solving becomes a satisfying challenge. i.e. crosswords or Sudoku. When it is in the context of an unwanted problem, you tense. Take driving, for instance; when you learn, you have to pay attention to so many things. It's overwhelming. You are tense. All aspects, checking the mirrors, changing gears, using the clutch, and the indicators, are stressful. But when you start getting used to driving, when you don't have to think and can do everything automatically, it becomes a habit, and you can relax. You can even take driving as a challenge and enjoy it, even to the point where some people go on a drive to relax. You are not dominated by all the demands. You are on top of it.

You know you have to do something, but it is not clear. You are not sure what you are supposed to do, and you don't have instructions. Yet you know you have to do it. To avoid the pressure, you don't want to add to the tension by having to think. So you engage in doing something that doesn't require thinking. You engage in what you know as knowing does not require any effort; knowing is habitual. You know your name, where you live, and what you know. You know how to get a pint of milk. No thinking involved. You know from experience. You know a beer, a biscuit, or switching on the TV will relax you. Whatever it is that you know will produce that effect. A cigarette for a smoker is the most reliable satisfaction they can get.

When people don't know how to react, what to think, or what to do, they sometimes act in an illogical, counterproductive way. Even when they realise what they are doing, they remain undeterred. They go in the wrong direction, realise it, but continue regardless. Why? Because the anxiety prevents them from thinking. They are not in control. It is the same reaction as humour. Something makes you laugh, and you have an uncontrolled reaction to what's happening. It's funny because it is not what it's expected. Maybe the change of context makes it funny. We have all seen those viral slapstick videos where someone riding a motorbike accelerates instead of braking and veers off into a field of cows.

I once was in a simulation game where people had to make critical decisions. They had to choose black or white, according to the criteria. Because they couldn't understand the problem but had to make a decision, they decided on random factors that had nothing to do with the matter at hand. They made decisions based on any reason that somehow made sense to them. For example, they picked black because their shoes were black or white because they liked white. I thought it was strange, but we all do it to a certain extent.

People may avoid thinking, but they have opinions. Opinions don't require thinking. It's what they know.

Whether it's the state of the planet, Brexit, or insecurity, we feel powerless to address the issue. It is too complex. Thinking about it is strenuous and overwhelming. We don't know what to do or how to decide. We have no suggestions for others or ourselves. So, as it is uncomfortable, we avoid thinking.

We only do it when it hits a critical threshold. This threshold is subjective. If we don't feel too bad, the threshold is lower.

It depends on how you see yourself in relation to life and how you experience the pressure. At the extreme end of the scale, a psychopath is not stressed. They don't think about consequences. They don't feel empathy for others or themselves. This lack of consideration makes decision-making easier, which is why we find them as leaders in the City. But when you are stressed, hopeless, or helpless, thinking is stressful in itself, so you avoid it and watch daytime TV instead. It is the equivalent of a baby sucking their thumb. It is an activity that reassures. It is not quite the nipple, but it is a substitute that will do. It brings comfort.

Notice the difference between a problem you want to resolve and one you don't.

First, think of a problem solving exercise you like. It could be sorting out books on the shelf, crosswords, or how to repair the situation.

The other could be something you have avoided, like talking to someone about a difference of opinion or fixing the leaking tap.

Notice the difference between an activity where you choose to think and one where you don't.

Background / foreground

When something stresses you, you are tempted instead to do something else, something pleasant. You move away from the painful and towards the pleasurable, or normal. You had a problem and now you have a solution. That is satisfying, and furthermore, that solution is pleasurable. However, there is a matter of considering just the moment or long term, what ultimately you should be doing. How effective is your 'coming back on track' mechanism?

What in retrospect you would call a bad habit, like daytime TV, spending time on the computer, or going out and getting drunk, is in line with the purpose for which you engage in the first place: feeling good, now. After all, you are doing something pleasant instead of that 'thing' that you should do that creates stress. You are actively avoiding something stressful by doing what you are doing, it is successful. It feels good. It fulfils its function.

What you ultimately have to do or be, the overall situation demanding your attention, or what your purpose should be, is in the background, whereas what you are currently doing, the enjoyable distracting activity you take part in, is in the foreground. So you may be aware of both and they are aligned and all is well, or they are not, and at some point, you feel bad as you are off track.

If the background and the foreground are aligned, you will feel good. You would be on purpose. For example, you have decided that you should find a companion, so you go to a social place where you can meet people. So the purpose and the activity you are now in are aligned. If the two are not aligned, for example, watching daytime TV when you should be doing your tax return, the incompatibility makes you feel bad.

You focus on the foreground, then the background, but not simultaneously, and you somehow feel guilty and ashamed about wasting time or not being able to control your behaviour, but it may not spur you into action. You would continue watching TV when you are supposed to do your tax return, with a sense of guilt. You sense that you are wasting time and feel bad. It would help if you had the ability to stabilise reality by being aware of both simultaneously.

Likewise, if you focus on the background, with no connection to the foreground, what you are doing, you will feel that you have good intentions but don't fulfil them. You may end up blaming yourself for being passive and unable to act. That is what happens to people with good intentions, such as being a good citizen or having a vision for helping the planet but don't do the first step. You may even have an idea, but you are long-sighted and can't see what is in front of you. Why deal with reality when you have a compelling dream?

Usually, you would be paying attention to the foreground, (what occupies you), but the rest, (the background), is not clear. If it was, you would become aware of wasting your time. You could see that you are doing this when you should be doing that. But what often happens is that people forget why they are there in the first place. Why do they forget? Do they lose sight of their purpose? It happens because the foreground is concrete, tangible, and perceptible. In contrast, the background is abstract and exists in the realm of ideas.

Think of the experiments developmental psychologists conduct with two-year-olds. They can have their marshmallow now, or if they wait five minutes, they can have two marshmallows. The object of their interest is there, tangible in front of them. They can see, smell, and almost taste it; it makes them salivate. The concept of delayed gratification is abstract. It requires an effort, a decision, or a strategy. Lots of kids demonstrate these personal strategies. They distract themselves with something else. They don't look at the tempting object. What you don't see ceases to exist.

Similarly, people have a mixed ability to think about the future. For some, it is easy and natural. For others, it is difficult or even impossible. In the same way, some people can look at the stars and make sense of them, and others find the whole thing a nebulous concept they can't grasp. It is not about intelligence. It is more akin to eyesight. It is about internal representation.

You may be aware of what to do but unclear on how to do it—for example, writing an essay. It is the background, but now that you have to initiate it, you don't know how to start or even continue; there is nothing in your foreground. So you postpone your anxiety by doing what you currently do for another five minutes, a well-known tactic for pupils and students throughout history. This is the major cause of procrastination.

You may have put yourself in the situation and did what is expected, but you forgot the purpose, so there is no feedback that spurs you forward. If you are unclear about your intention, your brain will revert to the normal state of affairs, waiting for instructions. You typically see that in bars or at parties. People go to socialise because there are other people, allegedly there for the same purpose, but they stay in their corner and may even feel intruded on if someone speaks to them. This is because they are not clear that their intention is to be social. They would automatically stay passive and feel lonely because they don't talk to anyone. And maybe to occupy themselves, they smoke or drink or check their phone to see if they get a message.

Then they return home and reflect on the evening as a dissatisfying outing. They blame the place for not being good or themselves for not acting, being shy, lacking confidence, etc. And because they cannot maintain the purpose in the background, when they are distracted by what is happening around them, the foreground, they repeat the same boring going out regularly.

They may drink too much, maybe because it was something to do, but it is at the detriment of having an interesting conversation with others. Or it may work, it makes them talkative, but now they have to be drunk to converse with others. The person they interact with experiences the same, and so they like each other. They get inebriated because they lost the background, leading to a short attention span and not thinking of consequences. But they now feel good because they are free and uninhibited, focusing only on the moment.

Being drunk or intoxicated reduces perspective drastically, making us feel good because of that; out of sight, out of mind. We went there for a purpose, meeting someone, but as we don't, drinking helps you forget what you are supposed to remember, and the conflicting pressure diminishes. End of the conflict of interest.

But we can also decide to intentionally reduce our scope to what we are currently doing to be present in what we are doing. For example, I don't want to check my emails when I am on holiday or I want to give my full, undivided attention to the person I am speaking to.

When you have no clear focus or alignment between the activity levels, you may be aware that you are doing a displaced activity. Maybe you would even be doing more of what is considered a waste of time. More bingeing because you feel bad for being fat: back to the start of the vicious circle. A solution to satisfy needs you don't understand.

At a physiological level, when you can't see, you tense your eyesight. However, when your vision is relaxed, you can see both foreground and background, but if you tense on either, you don't see the other. Martial artists, and to an extent all fighters, train to defocus so that they are not tracking one thing whilst something else is happening. On the other hand, magicians keep your attention purposefully on one aspect so that you miss what is happening elsewhere.

Think of the last time you intended to do something and got sidetracked.

Notice how you have lost your perspective. (e.g. you were going to talk to someone about something and got distracted and forgot). Is it a regular occurrence?

Compare it with a similar situation where you can maintain your perspective, e.g. staying on task when preparing a big presentation coming up at work. You are very clear about the intention; you don't let it dominate you but you set clear time aside to respond to the task fully

How do you maintain both foreground and background?

What is happening now, and what is your to-do?

Different levels

We often do things we like at one level but don't at another. For example, somebody feels bad about themselves because they are overweight. So they eat cake to feel better and indeed feel better when they eat. They may even feel better about their relationship with themselves because they treat themselves well.

When stressed, you tend to regress to a more childlike, hopeless person. From being a baby to growing up, most solutions to anxiety or feeling bad are about putting things in your mouth. It starts with a pacifier or your thumb, but the process is the same. Treating yourself to ice cream, wine, or whatever is your treat is an updated childish solution. You have probably witnessed what people do when pushing a pushchair, and their child starts to get cranky. They put something in the child's mouth. They can't whine if their mouth is full!

As the existentialist French philosopher Jean Paul Sartre said, "l'enfer c'est les autres" "Hell is the other". We judge ourselves by how others judge us. If it were not for others, we would just do as we please. Others often reflect a different part of ourselves. So, when the feel-good factor of eating sweet things is over, and we become aware of our bulge, usually because of the social context and what it means in terms of worth, we feel bad again. Nowadays, it's still possible to feel good because there is a momentum to validate being big. There are adverts on TV of happy women wearing plus-size fashion. We now belong to a part of society that accepts our size.

However, we are not in control. And that is bad in the context of society. To live in a society, its members need to be in control of themselves. Religion and culture provide the rules by which we are to conduct ourselves: How we solve issues, how we treat each other, or who we can get in a relationship with.

On one level, you feel good, on another, you feel bad. I took the example of food, but it could be any behaviour you engage in that you may feel guilty or ashamed about later. It can be a simple case of procrastinating doing your tax return or getting rid of the items in your wardrobe that are worn out or you never wear. It can also be something more chronic, like not exercising, changing your diet, stopping drinking, or smoking.

Life and problems are complicated because the issues are compound. For example, you feel good because you satisfy your craving, but bad because it's sugar, but good because chocolate tastes marvellous, but bad because you are on a diet, but good because you listen to what you want, but bad because you told others you were on a diet and if they see you eating chocolate, etc., etc...

Identify your own vicious circle of addiction to a behaviour or activity.

Identify the aspects of the activity that make you feel both good and bad.

Create a balance sheet and try to be as objective as you can.

You can either do one side at a time or flip-flop in a "yes but" approach.

The solution is the problem

Several implications result from this. One is that, as previously said, solutions often reinforce and even compound problems.

A client, Rob, reflected on the fact that he was popular because people around him got help or things from him. He came to the conclusion that it was not reciprocated and that he had few real friends. Realising this, he avoided people, but he became morose. He had been helpful all his life and got pleasure from being of service to others. Now he was stuck in a vacuum – but didn't know he was. Everyone has experienced a similar situation, letting go of something but not having something to replace it. It is not sufficient to just decide to change something. He had to put something else in place, even if it was space to think. But to replace a habit of a lifetime, he needed an equally powerful new habit.

Clients may want to develop a new habit or complete a task. They will see a therapist or a coach to help them. I have often witnessed that the therapist would work at managing the behaviour or an unwanted pattern, whereas the problem may be in terms of conflicting meanings. For example, a client might say, "I would like to be more productive at work, but they will take even more advantage of me if I do."

Some therapists may work on revealing repeated situations that have in common the feeling of hopelessness to find a theme, such as abandonment. They would seek a past event that triggered that feeling of hopelessness or any other version of what they felt as a child. The idea is to realise that you felt like that because you were five years old and didn't have the resources to deal with the situation. It is normal that what happened, happened. You were not in control. Now you are an adult and realise that you have the resources to resolve the problem. You have an 'ah-ha moment'. You are not a 5-year-old. You can care for yourself. You can move on; you are not stuck in the problem.

It can, in effect, reinforce the problem because when the high of having the insight fades away, the problem is ready to pounce again. I am not a five-year-old. I am an adult; an adult that feels hopeless. You were like this because you didn't know better. Now you know, and you are still like this. Until the next 'ah-ha moment,' and until hopelessness creeps back again. That 'ah-ha moment' also occurs because when you are liberated from the restriction, anything seems possible. But that feeling disappears when we are disconnected from that moment of realisation. There is no more feeling of possibility; now, it is just an idea, drained of its juicy potential. This is what happens to people who go on self-improvement/personal development workshops and have to return again and again to reconnect or hope that one day the feeling will stay permanent. Life becomes a roller coaster of ups and downs, joy and anguish, hope and despair.

People do not need to have a helper to achieve helplessness. They are quite happy doing it by themselves. On top of what was described previously, they can strive toward high standards. However, the expectations are so high that they come with doubts about whether they can meet those. Perfectionism is fertile ground for stress and worry.

What is a childhood event that shaped your life?

What elusive solution have you pursued that always seemed to be the solution yet does not solve your problem?

A good indicator may be the same type of self-help books or courses you buy.

Do you look for factors that influence your life beyond your control? i.e. astrology, to explain the way it is. (I have nothing against astrology!)

You are cursed - The stories that you tell yourself

When you have a feeling, you take it that it means that you are the description of that feeling. You feel hopeless, you are hopeless. You can put whatever terms would fit: Hopeless, helpless, a waste of time, not good enough, not smart enough, too sensitive, unlucky, cursed. The list is endless, but some descriptions would fit you more than others. It is you.

Counterexamples won't change things. If you feel unlucky in life, given a bad hand, born under the wrong stars, whatever someone could say about your blessings would not stick. It would even show you that nobody understands you and your situation. So not only are you cursed but alone. A counterexample, a break in your bad luck, may temporarily make you feel that it is over, but if another example occurs, then the certainty of the curse is reinforced.

You tried. There is no hope. You are doomed.

That is why we sometimes say that trying to get rid of the problem reinforces it.

Whatever level you are dealing with, it cannot be sorted in simple cause and effect, as in "you just have to do this." The problem may exist at a process level, with feedback loops reinforcing the way it is. A person with anxiety might be worried because they cannot see what they are worried about, for a good reason there may not be anything, no content to see.

Being worried and not knowing why would be increasingly worrying. The person, or a helper, may be looking for a tangible cause because it is common sense that there must be a reason. It is easy to speculate on what it could be and conclude that this must be 'it.' And when and a person comes up with an idea that they think is the right one, they feel good. The reason temporarily shuts down the feeling.

Whereas if they could realise that their worrying is based on the fact that there is an absence of something worrying them, and that is why they worry, the worrying could stop straight away.

For example, a person may be anxious because nothing is happening. They would try to make sense of feeling bad. They search through what happened recently and lock on to their friend Tom who has not returned their phone call. It is not the first time. Is he really a friend? Now they think they know why they feel bad. In reality, it may have nothing to do with Tom.

When a child is scared of the monster in the cupboard that he cannot see because the monster can make itself invisible, it's different because there is something identified to be worried about: a monster.

It could also be that the opposite feedback loops that should be there to create a virtuous circle are missing.

The more people try to figure their problem out, the more attention they pay to the state of their body, to the tension lets them know something is going on. They tense and go back to what they know: trying to understand with their analytical mind. It is the difference between man and animals. Animals deal with present reality, not unnecessarily concerning themselves about future scenarios that don't exist and therefore can't do anything practical about it. Man may be more intelligent, but they worry.

Einstein knew that when he needed to relax his mind, he would let go of resolving the equations of the universe and instead play the violin. The Eureka moment would then come to him when the tension had receded. Of course, most people have their own way of engaging in physical activity to relax the mind.

How do you convince yourself that you are (whatever judgment you give yourself)?

First, notice the feeling and the judgment.

Notice that as a pattern, you can't distinguish between the cause and the effect.

Like Einstein, you probably have your own way of getting rid of the feeling that makes you rigidly think in a certain way. What is it?

Is there hope, Doctor?

Controlling the environment

Seneca, the Roman philosopher, explained that in infancy, we discover that the source of the satisfaction of our needs lies beyond our control and that the world is unreliable in supplying our desires. So, we have to address that. We control the means of making our future safer by developing a lifestyle, securing a job and a roof, finding a person who commits to loving us, and having a few activities and things that make us feel good.

As man evolved, he created a home that he decorated, as in caves. Then he moved plants near his house so he didn't have to go far to find nutrition. Similarly, for animals, he put an enclosure so that he didn't have to go on dangerous hunts. He just had to defend his patch from marauders. He could control the supply more. Then he exchanged and bartered.

He then lived in bigger communities and started to specialise in what he could trade. It started as physical objects, such as meat or tools, to things more and more abstract, such as hedge funds.

Like your ancestors before you, you were encouraged to do well at school so that you would be able to find a good job. With a good job comes financial security so that you can plan and support a family. You have a pension for old age, a mortgage to afford a house, and savings for future eventualities. Your lifestyle supports your feeling of safety.

You exert as much control over life as you can. However, if you lose your job, are made redundant, or your life partner leaves you, your life collapses, and stress returns.

Anxiety is a constant in life. The harsh conditions of the wilderness and harsh weather when there is nothing to eat have been replaced with an all-year supply and artificial food, but modern life replaced it with constant pressure and demands. Artificial lights created an environment to be able to work constantly. We started by controlling the environment, now it is unclear to what extent the environment is controlling us.

> Look around your life, from your job, friends, and the objects around you, and notice how they are representative of your control in life.
>
> You can either do it physically, sitting where you live, looking around, or thinking about your setup.

I believe

The Greek philosopher Socrates tried to get everybody he met to reflect on the premises of their lives. Tirelessly, he challenged what his compatriots knew, the assumptions of the beliefs they held without questioning them. Socrates annoyed people and was judged. The verdict was that he was disturbing the way things had always been. He was condemned to death. Athenians didn't like that their established beliefs and customs were questioned by a heretic using rhetoric.

Similarly, we don't like to be challenged about what we know. We create our moral environment with our ideas, conclusions, and thinking. We have a lot invested in what we have accumulated and would find the questioning of what we know as offensive.

We don't like others doing it. We don't like doing it to ourselves, especially when stressed. So we have a need to defend our beliefs. It is not about the validity of the argument. It is about defending the identity, the integrity of the identity of what we know.

We protect the benefits we gain from having our beliefs or attitudes. One of the benefits is that we belong to a group of people that share this belief.

If challenged, it is felt like a personal attack on the group we belong to. In return, we attack the other camp's identity. We saw that in the Brexit debate or with the way Donald Trump operated. Remainers and Brexiteers didn't always address the issues discussed but the personal character of the individual confronting their viewpoint. It is simpler and diverts the attention away from the issues. It is not about trying to find a consensus towards the truth but about trying to demean the other side. The British Parliament and political parties operate on that basis.

We control our moral environment with our beliefs. In that environment, we feel at home. We belong. Whatever doesn't fit is rejected, especially when we are stressed. We have little tolerance for anything that rocks the boat. It does not matter that it is sound, logical, or factual.

It is the same as with food. We exchange ideas or information like we share food. If you are not used to this kind of diet, it is a shock to the system. An idea needs to be chewed and digested to be part of the system. Beliefs are so integrated into our habits and behaviours that we may, on the surface, agree with the argument, but if it doesn't fit in, it is ejected. It is like a mental immune system reacting against an attack. Furthermore, we live in a household and always eat the same food together. As a result, we can suffer from malnutrition of ideas.

Long live the status quo.

Take anything that you believe strongly about. It could be religious, political, social, or cultural. For example, if you hear someone saying, "Women and children shouldn't eat until the man eats first." Notice your reaction. If a person were to tell you it is the right way, you would not be neutral and listen constructively to their argument about why it is the right way but would feel they are attacking your ways.

Pick whatever is relevant to you, in whatever context.

It may be easier to think of other people doing it, defending their point of view, before you find your own example.

Because we can

Another aspect is important when we are talking about engaging in activities with little thinking involved. Often because I am a psychotherapist, people ask me, "why does so and so behave the way that they do?" My first answer is often, "Because they can."

Being in the 'can mode' is about not thinking of consequences. For example, it is said that when parents disapprove of what their kids are doing, they think only of the consequences; the children just think of the excitement of doing the action.

In the natural world, we can observe juvenile animals, including us humans, run and jump because it brings thrills and excitement. As a child, you don't run because you have to go somewhere. You run because you like it. You've got legs, you've got space; like Forrest Gump; you run because you can.

Whereas later, the mature animal only moves for a reason; unbounded energy versus wisely spent energy.

When you are a child, every performance is a way of testing your boundaries and your capabilities. You do it because you can. Do you remember as a child or teenager doing something daring? There may have been fear involved, but you pushed the boundaries by setting how far you could go. For us boys, in summer, at the river, it was diving from difficult places or in as shallow water as possible. There was excitement, fear, social recognition, pride, and belonging to those who can and not to those who can't.

Then comes a point when you think this particular behaviour is outdated, and it is time to move on. Examples would be a toddler being on the potty and wanting to go on the normal toilets, or a boy or girl sucking their thumb and discovering at nursery school from others that it's babies who do that, so they stop.

It continues in the adolescent years, with the increasing pressure of having to prove yourself in groups and an obsession with how you look to others. As a teenager, the pressure to conform is immense. I remember the distress of my nephew when I suggested that we go to the supermarket to buy the trainers he needed. It was a tragedy for him not to have the right, trendy trainers his peers would approve of. Supermarket trainers were unthinkable. First and foremost, it was not shoes he needed, it was the right shoes. It was status.

It is very relevant when listening to someone because you need to take into account what stage they are at in their life in order to make sense of what is happening to them. They may engage in behaviours where there is no reason for it. Just because they can, or if there is a reason, they can't explain it. "It's like this... because it's like this. That's it."

If you pay attention to adverts on TV, you can see those principles. For products aimed at youth, what is usually portrayed is energy, speed, going beyond limits, and involves others.

Whereas for adults and the elderly, the adverts are explicit. They are factual and informative. It is mainly about preparing for the future, protecting children, using cream to prevent ageing, or sorting out the burden of funerals before you die.

Even if it is the same product category, like cosmetics, the body sprays for teenage boys are about impact and results. If you wear it, you can get the girls.

On the other hand, cosmetic adverts aimed at women tend to describe the problem realistically and explain how they work with pseudo-scientific terms. For men, it explains that three blades on your razor shave better than one. The first blade is to pull the hair out of the follicle, etc.

For a teenager, the meaning of failure and judgement from peers, with the shame associated with it, is huge. For adults, in some contexts, when their life depends on social approval, it is too. So the need to belong and not be ostracised is vital. And a lot of behaviours that people engage in are to conform to the norm. Or, like rebels, it is to belong to a selective group of reactionary, free-thinking people. Not belonging to the mainstream, but nevertheless belonging to a group that exists in relation to the main group.

What is dictated by others slowly becomes what is dictated by the self. There is no clear difference between the two. Rules and directives are assimilated into the person's system.

That 'can mode' can also be observed when testosterone is high. The male of the species, in animals, including humans, can engage in dangerous behaviours to prove themselves. The behaviour of drivers in some countries, where they overtake on the inside lane, outside lane, drive bumper to bumper at Grand Prix speed, is something you have probably experienced, regrettably, and they do it just because they can; and get a thrill.

Every man and woman have contexts in their life where they are more likely to be in the 'can' mode.

Of course, despite a general tendency of being mainly in capability mode when you are young, and towards a mainly meaningful mode when you are more mature, the two are not mutually exclusive. Like yin and yang, they both encompass the other. It's a combination of both. You start with mainly engaging in behaviour because you can, and with some meaning, usually a simple meaning. For instance, trendy trainers mean respect. Then, later in life, it is mainly meaning, with some capability. Meaning being more connected to everything in life, more big scale, spiritual, beyond the ego self. By ego self, I mean the sense of self-importance, of being at the centre of attention, needy. And the capability aspect is more connected to mastery, the pleasure of being good at something effortlessly.

And although it is a general linear progression, there are also times of revisiting. It's cyclical, like the man in a midlife crisis, when he has to check whether he's still got it with younger women. But generally, as we age, most of life is not concerned with proving oneself professionally, physically, or intellectually. First of all, because we know where we stand, but also because it is more about finding meaning and a sense of purpose in one's life.

Whether a person is young or old, they still have energy fluctuation each day. These are called the circadian rhythm. They are affected by digestion slump, hunger, rest or sleep deprivation; or because they may be sick, depressed, or exhausted. All those factors will greatly influence whether a person would be in the 'can mode' or 'meaning mode'.

If you take the apprenticeship of martial arts or any other discipline, the student would learn the basics at the beginning. They would enjoy pushing boundaries, developing their skills, and having a go every time they see an opportunity. It is reactive and exciting. They would throw a punch because they can. It works, or it doesn't.

With experience, and when they have nothing to prove, the emphasis moves to mastery. From brawlers, they become zen masters. In mastery, there is no losing or winning. Instead, there is control; control over what is happening, how one is reacting, and control over self. It is equally true for fighting as it is for ballet dancing or playing poker.

For many clients, their issue revolves around their capability to do or not do something. By the end of our work together, it has shifted to a more meaningful frame. A good example of that is addiction or compulsion. You stop doing something like drinking or overeating or worrying, because we have worked on the awareness of the issue and also on the emergence of meaning that was not there initially. It may be because we have worked on it directly, a meaning that was not there and now is, or it may have come up as a result of weakening the hold of the addiction and compulsion. Being freed from it allows the meaning to grow.

Pick examples in your life of doing things because you can.

Do not have any judgement associated with it, no intention to change anything.

Just become aware that you do things without consciously thinking about them.

On autopilot

Most of our behaviours, habits, and problems are in place because we don't review how they work. They are based on associations that we don't check, even if those associations may not serve us.

Most people unconsciously associate sugar and energy. It is not just the sugar itself. The idea of sugar also gives you energy. People know that about holidays. The travel agent would tell them the holidays start when you buy your ticket, and to a certain extent, it is true. The satisfaction of the need starts when you think of the solution. This is the case when it is in the 'can mode,' and the need/solution is fused, not sequential. The solution implies the need. You see a nice cake; it creates the hunger for it.

As you get the good effect beforehand, you seldom review the behaviour. This is because the brain forms an unconscious association between sugar and energy, or alcohol and relaxing. It precedes the unwanted after-effects. But you only think of the idea of a thing rather than the whole sequence. So you would have to train it to associate with the unwanted effect if you wanted to change it. You would need to do that consciously and repeatedly. That is why it is worth thinking through the sequence to consider the consequences.

Typically, I would only exercise if I feel I have the energy for it, whereas it is doing exercise that gives me energy. For example, I think I should go running, but just thinking about putting on my shoes and going running, I feel I don't have the energy, so I can't go and don't go. In contrast, for yoga, when I have to go to a class, I may not have energy now, but I know that at the end of the class, I will have energy. In other words, I think it through, even though it is mostly unconscious and streamlined because I have repeatedly verified it. So I go, regardless of how I feel in the moment.

Have you ever noticed that hunger disappears as soon as food is on its way, even before you eat it? You are hungry, so you feel tension. Just the idea that you are going to eat relieves the tension of the frustration. Not just food, the idea of something happening often begins to take effect even before it happens in reality.

"I go to the fridge to get something to eat. I open the door and wonder why I did that. I didn't particularly want something from the fridge. My stomach made me do it. There is always something to eat there." We are ruled by automatisms without us controlling them consciously. The fridge example helps clients see that their automatic pilot is powerful and they need to overcome their conditioning. By developing their awareness, their sense of control increases.

So we take their habitual actions and identify what they want control over. They grasp the difference between intention and action. They realise that they create reality. They say they will and do it and feel the energy of will. They practise energizing the intention. In the instance of being pulled by the fridge like an automat, they would realise it is happening, realise that they don't want to. They realise that they want to say no. They develop the will for it, and verify that they feel great having said no to the fridge. They develop choice. It is similar to developing gratitude. When you practise gratitude, you see evidence of good things in your life. You are more connected to yourself and others. You belong more. You relax. Awareness of being on autopilot has similar effects. You regain control. You can use automatism to serve you rather than being used by it.

Some people are shy and can't talk to someone because they don't know what to say; it creates anxiety. However, once they have spoken to them, they can talk about anything. In their mind, they're now a friend, so they can talk to them easily. The association is an automatic, unconscious relief.

Most fears and phobias work because you don't think them through. You may think you do because you think of the consequences, like "the spider could bite me." In reality, you don't think them through. It stops at the level of having no control rather than having control. As in, "So what would happen if the spider bites me. What would I do then?" If you think it through, the fear shrivels, like the size of the spider!

Most of what we do operates out of habit. Most of what we do is unconscious. The process of doing something has been established through practice, learnt, and we don't need to think about it any more. If the experience was intensely emotional, you learn quickly. No need for repetition. That's what often happens with a phobia. A one-time experience, and you react straight away. Most of the time, for other behaviours, you require repetition, like when you tie your shoelaces. It is just part of a practice, the practice of putting your shoes on. The same goes for more complex behaviours, like forecasting stock exchange variations, made of repeated smaller learning experiences. Even when you speak or write, you don't have to think about how to do it. Right now, as I write my ideas, I think them, but my fingers automatically type what I think. Any task has a part of conscious attention and a part of unconscious processing. Even when thinking, I think of the content, but the process of thinking is automatic.

Most behaviours come from satisfying a need or solving a problem. The solution we found works, so we tend to use it again. But sometimes more than we should, and to other problems where they don't fit.

Some problems can be addressed more directly by looking at them as habits. For example, habits you may have had at a time in your life, like sucking your thumb or smoking, may have been good at one point but may not be now. Or they may be good in certain circumstances and certain quantities but not in others. For example, it's ok to have a drink at the end of the working day, but not ten pints, or to drink alcohol first thing when you wake up.

One may drink excessively because they discovered that alcohol relaxes them and makes them forget their problems.

And over time, they took too much of the solution, developed habits and a life around it. They made drinking friends. They are part of a drinking establishment where everybody knows their name. And now they still have their original practical problems, plus alcoholic issues!

Some habits like smoking, for instance, may have changed because they are outdated. It may have changed because the context has changed, like being pregnant. It may have changed because you have evolved. These are all variations on the same theme: it was a good idea at the time, but now it is time to move on.

That is why exploring the past and uncovering the reasons is a tortuous and hit-and-miss process. The ego is apt at making up stories where it is at the centre of what's happening and becomes the hero, even in hardship and suffering. We can spend an endless number of sessions exploring your creativity in connecting meanings and implications and developing themes. It is rewarding to emulate Miss Marple, eliciting facts and meanings about your life, or making it up as it comes like Captain Jack Sparrow. It feels like we achieve something, but all that leads to is practising creativity, not solving a problem.

My role as a therapist is to open concepts, beliefs, and preconceptions, for reviewing them and checking their usefulness, and once updated, close them again to be stored as concepts, beliefs, and preconceptions. The result is that the client has fewer conflicts in how they function. What has been brought to consciousness, laid bare, can go back into the subconscious as part of the undergrowth of meanings.

Most therapies can be on a scale where two dynamics take place. One side is about the relationship between therapist and client; the other side is about problem solving. Some people go to see a therapist for years. They have someone they trust which is an exception in their life. Trust may have been upset in their childhood or not nurtured. With the therapist, they can reveal themselves, talk about themselves, and learn to trust. Others have a problem that they want to resolve, quickly if possible. They are not there to find a friend or gossip about themselves. It depends on what the client wants. Clients are anywhere between those two dynamics. Both are important.

People have a contextualised problem, such as a problem with a specific person, but they think they have a problem with people in general and look for a solution for dealing with people. If you have a problem with Tom or Sarah, It doesn't apply to another person because the problem with that person is specific. There is a danger in going into a generalisation of the problem and of the solution. If you deal with a specific problem, you keep it in that context, and you are more resourceful in dealing with it. So that when you act, you have feedback on what you have done, which would not be the case if the problem is generalised. You also don't subsequently go around trying to gather evidence to back your theory about problems with people. The territory is always specific.

Think of someone who has developed an excessive solution, or a solution that works for other problems where it doesn't fit the situation.

For example, a drink at the end of the day to relax, but now has developed a drinking habit or someone who is admired because they talk straight, but doesn't know when to be diplomatic.

When you have done that, start to wonder about your own examples of a solution that initially worked, so you tend to use it again, more than you should, and to other problems where they don't fit.

Notice those actions you may want to review from being on automatic pilot, to regain some control over.

Notice your initial intention and how it went.

Regain control of your life

The 'can mode'

One night I was eating delicious salted caramel ice cream whilst watching TV. When the movie finished, I cleared the side table. I took two empty pots of ice cream to the bin. Putting the pots in the rubbish bin, I was aware that was greedy. I was a glutton. Plus, it was going to make me fat and a huge amount of sugar. Terrible. Prior to doing that, I had the intention of losing the excess fat around my belly. I was fascinated by how I did that. So, I went back to the sequence that led to the crime, analysed it, and came to a conclusion:

There are two modes: Can and meaning. In the 'can mode' I identified three dynamic aspects: availability, permission, and pleasure. All are unconsciously present.

I invite you to either take the example of eating ice cream, if you like ice cream, or any indulgence of yours, to check the elements below. Keep your example in mind and then continue reading.

Availability

There was a succession of events that led to being able to have the ice cream. First, it was available in the shop, then it was available in the freezer. Then once open, after each spoonful, there was still some ice cream in the pot. Even when I finished eating one, there was still another pot in the freezer. There was still space in my stomach for more. So I started a new pot of ice cream.

When we go shopping, either we do it mindfully, with a list of ingredients we need, like my mum does, or like most of us, in the convenience shops that have sprung in all the high streets, we look around and put things in the basket. Because it is there. Plus, who can resist buy one get one free. We do it because we can.

Now before you get disgusted with someone who would eat two tubs of ice cream in one go, think about how astonished and repulsed the people from Southern Europe are by the English behaviour of drinking several pints of beer in one evening.

Since I discovered the working of the 'can mode,' I have stopped buying ice cream! I look at the "2 for £5" and laugh at the luring attempt.

Permission

Implicitly, there is an authorisation: "Go on, have another one." It feels like a child giving another child a treat. When someone is conflicted, it is as if they have two parts of them in conflict. One that says I would like to and the other saying I shouldn't. In the case of the 'can mode,' there isn't any of that. You do it completely willingly. You give yourself permission, even if it is implicit.

When you give yourself permission, it releases tension. It gives choice and freedom. It also ends the tension of having to choose between yes and no. There is now a direction. Additionally, there is an element of good relations. Instead of being conflicted and split, permission helps to be at one with yourself. We usually give permission explicitly to others, more rarely to ourselves.

When I presented this can model to an audience, one participant stated that at his workshops, biscuits are made available to participants, but if you put a smiley or a sad face above the plate of biscuits, it dramatically affects the consumption. With the happy face, they ate lots of biscuits; with the sad one, they were restricted. They would take a biscuit with their coffee but wouldn't munch their way through several. Their inner permission is restricted by the disapproving smiley.

In England, putting a policeman cut-out in shops dramatically cuts theft. The image of a representative of the law affects the permission to steal. In other countries, they place policemen cut-outs on the side of the road for speed limitation.

Pleasure

There is pleasure in doing the action. The pleasure makes you want to continue the action. You are in the moment in the 'can mode.'

As I don't measure hormones, I can only speculate that the dopamine and endorphin levels are high. You are bonding with yourself. There is a rush of chemicals in the brain, and when you are happy, you are more likely to give yourself permission.

The three aspects are intertwined, indissociable, and mutually benefiting each other. Giving permission gives pleasure. The opportunity that is there, available, means you give yourself the permission to go for it. The pleasure continues as long as you continue. "It's there, it's good, go on." "It's good, go on, it's there." "Go on, it's good, it's there." "Alright then. I will." I could have called it the enticing siren mode.

We can differentiate two meanings of can: can of availability and can of capability. Availability because it's there. Like you can eat the ice cream because you have it.

Capability because you are capable of eating both tubs. It is reactive because it is in contrast to cannot. It implies you enjoy pushing boundaries. It means you are capable of more, which means you enjoy availability. It becomes recursive.

Time disappears.

In the 'can mode,' there is no judgement, as there is no comparison. No good and bad; worse or better. It is what it is. Judgements may come later, in retrospect, but during that phase, you are entirely present in the moment. But not consciously, that's the whole point, because it is habitual, you don't need to be conscious. Because you are in the moment, you are actively avoiding worries.

You are in the habitual mode, so the levels of behaviour, meaning, who you are, are all aligned. It has been established through successful repetition.

Let's take the example of a pastime, like playing Solitaire, the card game. The three elements of the 'can mode' are present. You know how to play the game, it is familiar, it is available. Once you have decided to play a game, you have implicitly given yourself permission. You chose to do it because it is pleasurable. It could be a pleasant mixture of relaxation and tension in this challenge. When you align all the cards, you feel a sense of success and achievement; you won. You feel good, so you give yourself permission to play another game. You have time, and it is available. If you play on the computer, there is a button that makes another game available. It is easy. If you are stuck or lose, the objective is to feel good, so you play again. All the factors are there to enjoy the activity. The same factors are at work for someone betting big sums at the casino. This is also the case for any activity you like doing, even if considered to be mundane chores, like ironing or vacuuming. They can all be in the 'can mode' and have those three factors present.

It is very useful to put as much of your actions into the 'can mode' because of the absence of critical judging, and to do the things that you do mindlessly, more effectively.

In contrast, for addiction or unwanted habits, becoming aware of the permission, availability, and pleasure aspects helps to dismantle them more easily. Many clients I have explained the model to have reported they are now in control of unwanted habits because they are aware of how they work. You can disconnect an addiction by tweaking each or all three aspects: availability, permission and pleasure.

We describe the stages of learning a skill as going from unconscious incompetence to unconscious competence. Think juggling, for instance. You were not even aware of some of the aspects of the skill and realise as you try that it is difficult. You are conscious of your incompetence. Having practised, you can do it, but it takes all your concentration. You have to think, maybe explain to yourself what needs to happen. "Put your hand underneath the ball to receive it. Send the other ball up with the other hand". You become consciously competent. You can do it. After a while, through repetition, it becomes easy. You don't need to think about it. It's automatic. You are now unconsciously competent. Through repetition, you become better at it, so you can be even more in the 'can mode.' You do things mindlessly more effectively when you are in the 'can mode.'

Animals are in 'can mode.' They interact with their environment in a harmonious way. They are driven by instinct. They can do what they need to do and, throughout life, develop experience, but they don't get stuck in plans that don't work. They may analyse situations and strategise, like when a group of predators approach a herd, but it is never disconnected from reality. It is trial and error but never ending in a "failure" or frustration. When they display unnatural behaviours, it is usually because they live with humans.

For example, the safari guide can interpret when the impalas run because they can and when it is meaningful. Because the main thing in the bush is to avoid a predator. All animals take their cue from other animals. They are oblivious to other grass eaters, except when they display a different behaviour; then, they are on alert. To stay alive in the African bush, you have to be mindful. If the wildebeest flees, so do the zebras, the antelopes, and the giraffes. They don't start to ponder the meaning of it.

Most of what we do is unconscious, and hopefully so. Because the effort required to be aware of everything is taxing. You need the right effort of awareness, tension, and relaxation. So you leave it to the unconscious to balance optimally for it to work. However, there are too many things we leave to the unconscious when we could do with a bit more awareness. Being mindful of not eating ice cream because it makes you fat, for example.

Being aware of the permission, availability, and pleasure aspects helps to dismantle an addiction more easily.

Think of an unwanted habit.

Notice those three dynamics at work.

Become aware of how they work.

The 'meaning mode'

In the chapter on autopilot, we saw that we did not need to think most of the time because things, activities, and sensations came with their own meaning. Here we are going to look at it from another angle. The fact that our compulsion to give meaning to our experiences makes it difficult to be objective.

Things are not just as they are. They are meaningful. Consider the incredible phenomena of reading and understanding the words that you are currently reading. If it was written in Chinese characters (unless you are able to transcribe them), they would not make any sense. Whereas now, reading this text stimulates your thinking. Can you imagine being able to glide your finger across a series of tactile dots on a Braille page and make sense of it as you do reading this page?

Even sounds. I like listening to foreign languages and marvel at the fact that, for me, they are random sounds. Whereas for another person, they are organised in a language. It's magical. A musician can read a score and hear music, whereas those black symbols clinging to the lines are meaningless to me.

We talk about thoughts and emotions as distinct, like you think of a thought, and it creates an emotion. In reality, they are not as distinct and mechanical. It is a much more fluid blend. Your thinking has a feel, an emotion, which can be subtle. That is the attraction of poetry.

The picture of a laughing child automatically comes with a warm feeling, whereas a picture of Donald Trump, Putin or the North Korean dictator, Kim Jong-Un, provokes another feeling.

When we relate to an object, person, or event, there is usually an emotional charge associated with it. Many objects in your house are symbolic and evocative.

The object and the meaning are intertwined. You can't see a fluffy duvet without thinking of comfort. You don't see a cake, you see a delicious cake. The deliciousness automatically comes with that cake.

That is what advertising achieves, associating a product with an emotional response. Most of the time, the product and the associated response are not related. There may be nothing much to a product that is different from the competition. There is nothing much to a shampoo compared to another. So, it is associated with your self-worth or a chocolate box with being a man of mystery. There are even adverts now that are so subtle that they don't mention the product, just the brand and an experience. It's the evocative effect.

The emotional charge associated with objects is also applicable to thinking. You heard someone saying, "The organisation is going to close my branch," and you say that is a scary thought because hearing it caused you dread. Thinking about doing your tax return, exercising, or doing a spring cleaning, can cause you to feel bad. You are going to postpone as much as you can, because you avoid feeling bad. But other activities don't cause you issues, because they are neutral or you think mainly about the positive aspects. Like if you exercise on a regular basis, your brain will be primed with the feel-good effect of having exercised. Or going to a social event, you are excited because you know that the people there are your friends. The thought of this party is automatically associated with feeling good.

Anything which is happening happens within a frame of meaning. When you change the frame, you change reality.

It is said that a frog would starve to death because it cannot see flies that don't move, even if there were plenty around. We are not dissimilar. All of us have objects or ideas no longer connected to their original meaning because of habituation, because we take them for granted, because of a state like sadness or depression. Things, activities, people, and relationships, over time, become static and disconnected, and we starve. What made them interesting, their value, has disappeared. Unless, of course, you practise being aware of their value, like regularly having gratitude. A friend, Shaheen, always acknowledges some positive aspects whenever he meets someone. We, humans, are social animals; therefore, we operate on reciprocity. You scratch my back, I scratch yours. It reinforces bonds and makes you feel good, both giving and receiving something we value.

The French say "L'argent ne fait pas le bonheur". "Money does not make people happy." If it's disconnected from its possibility, wealth is meaningless; worthless. Whereas when people win a money prize on a TV programme, they are overjoyed and excited. They know how they are going to spend it: a holiday with friends, staying in a beautiful place with their loved ones, or giving to charity. It has a felt value. It is imbued with a felt sense of possibility and benefits.

People who engage in addictive behaviour have a short loop between the benefit of the behaviour and the act. They get pleasure in the activity, not about its further meaning or the consequences of it. For example, people with a drinking problem are unable to think beyond drinking, which makes them feel good now. They are not thinking of the consequences. In any case, thinking about the consequences would make them feel bad, so they would need a drink to feel good.

That's why people figuring out their purpose find it energising. They are now connected to the rest of their life. They have a sense of direction. It is being made dynamic through the process of induction and deduction. It's alive. But when that purpose is a product, has become a concept, it's sterile, disconnected, meaningless. It is like a fly that is not moving.

Both objects and ideas are subject to an inevitable deterioration of their meaning, or rather the aliveness of their meaning. For example, you have pictures or souvenirs from people or holidays, but over time you stop seeing them. Even bad things will slowly disappear if they are not maintained actively.

There is pleasure and excitement in coming up with an idea. When it cools down, though, it is just an idea. It is not connected to what made it interesting. It is more to do with the process than the content. Creation gave it life; conceptualisation killed it. But, like fire, we can re-ignite it by talking about it. It is what makes the difference between someone who tells a joke and laughs whilst telling it and someone who would just repeat it by remembering the detail of it. The first one is funny, and the latter is not.

Similarly, when learning in life, we have an experience, and we come to a conclusion. It is fruitful, even if the experience was a negative one. We still come to a conclusion, but when the conclusion is solely conceptual, it is devoid of richness, of aliveness. A complex situation is reduced to a label.

Our thinking happens in a dynamic flow. Often it is obscure, incomprehensible to us, like when someone bursts into tears when you talk about the weather. It can even be confusing for the person themselves. We tend to listen to what someone is saying at face value, but for the person talking, it is connected to everything else in their life and loaded with meanings.

When questioning someone or oneself, the process of questioning and answering makes what was unconscious conscious. Meanings emerge, and strings of meanings unfold. Up to a certain point, some aspects can't easily come to awareness.

People may react against being questioned, as with the example of my nephew and buying supermarket trainers. It was loaded with meaning. He was outraged at the idea of buying them there and distraught when having to justify why trainers from the supermarket were a no-no. When not knowing, people often stress, get angry, and react negatively. In some cultures, asking a question to someone who may not know the answer makes them look stupid. Losing face is a taboo in Eastern cultures. That is why Asian students coming to Britain to learn English are the quietest ones in the class.

We saw that being in 'can mode' is being in the present. Meaning tends to be outside a specific time. It's timeless, general, and unspecified. "It's terrible, greedy, gluttonous. Sugar makes you fat. What kind of person would do that?"

We are ruled by rules and the way things should be. They are stored in our subconscious. You can bring them out into consciousness, to a certain extent, and discuss them rationally once exposed. But there would come a point where you need careful guiding, a deep meditative, or a trance state to uncover what would otherwise upset you because they are so charged with emotional meaning.

It is like culture. We do things because it is the way things are done. It is tradition. We can't easily justify them; they are like water to the fish. When you immerse yourself in another culture, then maybe you can have access to the deeper layers of your own culture. When you live abroad, by comparing the way you do things there, in your country of origins, and here, where you live, you realise that rules are constructed, subjective, and man-made.

A friend from Iran who lived here in the UK realised that she could not return to the imposition of rules that she had detached herself from. She could not be with people who think it's the way it is, that's it. She would question established rules or struggle to abide by them. Then she would be in conflict with the people around her. She would not belong.

I have a Japanese friend who is so conditioned by her Japanese culture that she struggles with anything different. Some people are so boxed in their culture, their own or country's culture, that for them, it is impossible to consider an alternative to the ways things are.

It makes things simple to follow rules. Take a game, you don't question the rules but the application of them. No footballer would say the game has to stop when the ball has gone over the line, but they would dispute that it had. Footballers are already quite petulant. Could you imagine if during matches, players would argue about the way the game should be played?

Your own culture is unconscious, in the same way as your community culture. You do it because that is the way you do it. You react when your unwritten rules and regulations are not respected. Like when we think strangers are stupid because they don't do as we do. I can't help judging and getting annoyed at people who keep sniffling next to me on public transport instead of using a tissue to blow their nose. In my culture, when your nose is runny, you need to blow it in a tissue, not let it run or sniff continuously. For others, collecting mucus in a handkerchief and putting it in a pocket is abhorrent.

Some of those rules and meanings that make us react are just for a specific time. Like for teenagers who become ashamed of their parents. I see on public transport pupils lovingly saying goodbye to their parents when they go to school and a couple of years later being embarrassed by them. A friend related this story when we were discussing the topic amongst friends: "It was my son's birthday. We were at the bowling alley. I was swaying side to side to the song "Dancing Queen". My daughter came out of the toilets, saw me on the other side of the room, and striding to me as soon as she could, she intensely whispered in my ear and walked off "Can you just never do that again!"

Young people tend to struggle with interpretation, trying to navigate, making sense of life, and the incongruities and paradoxes of the adult world. Whereas when people mature, they learn to accept the reality of life; it is the way it is. They become aware and appreciative of simple things. Not what it means, but the experience of it. Happy people appreciate simplicity, whereas people who are concerned with what it all means are missing out on what is in front of them.

We can't help it. We live in a sea of meanings. Everything is meaningful, connected in an infinite complex system. It is good to remind ourselves of that, even to question those meanings in a constructive way, rather than always being reactive to interpretations and implications. Without questioning the foundation of our worrying, it continues.

Think of an idea that you thought was brilliant at the time you conceived it, and then over time, it lost its interest.

Look at objects in your house that were so precious at the time you put them on the shelf and now don't see any more.

Think of something that bothers you.

What if that meaningfulness lost its potency like it did for the objects or ideas?

If you find it difficult, just know that not now, but in the future, it may.

'Is' and 'should be'

We are constantly comparing what 'is' and what 'should be'. In fact, it is the basis of our neurological functioning, always comparing nothing happening and something happening. For example, human eyes make saccadic movements to build a mental map. What we perceive is difference and change, similarly with physical sensations. What the polymath Gregory Bateson described as news of a difference. We react to what is there, like a radar. A radar resonates to something concrete that bounces back.

When you think something is going to happen, but it does not, you experience tension. It should happen, and it is not. You are stuck in this comparison. It is wrong. It is that conclusion that feeds back into that tension and drives what is being compared.

In social interactions, the gap between what should be happening and it is not, translates as a need for understanding and reassurance. It helps to appease that tension. If that sounds too abstract, try this: when someone asks you a question, look at them and don't answer straight away. They will try again, ask differently, or make non-verbal signals that they expect an answer, like raising eyebrows. There is a need for completion.

When you are out of breath, it is not as it should be. It's wrong. You want to breathe in more, you want to breathe out more too. You are constantly fluctuating between what 'is' and what 'should be', between it's OK and it's too much or not enough. Try it for yourself now. Breathe in and don't breathe out. Notice what happens. Feel the anxiety of something should be happening and it's not.

People are aware of what is happening to them, but not how. They experience distress and worry, not that they are comparing what 'is' and what 'should be'.

Some people feel a longing for a life they're not living. They know that the current one is not satisfying. They don't have the perspective to see that they are comparing their life to the life they should have had. They may, for example, find themselves emotional when watching someone else's life. If they check it out, they find that the idealised life is not fulfilling either. They can't find happiness in the current state of affairs or the ideal one and become depressed.

People are stuck because they need feedback. When depressed, they feel like they are in a bubble. Their thinking is limited to the confine of this bubble. There is no perspective to compare to. It is a system feeding on itself. So they lack the comparison between what 'is' and what 'should be', the tension that would make them react.

Hopefully, you are not anxious or depressed. You are blissful, fulfilled, appreciating the beauty and sweetness of the moment. May it last...

May it last? That presupposes it won't (another comparison). But it should!(another comparison!)

As long as you are alive, life has a habit of throwing unexpected spanners in the works.

Whether aware or not, we also compare what is to what could be. But sometimes 'could' may not stay 'could' for long. It has a tendency to become 'should'.

Many moments in life are experienced as 'it is' or as 'should be', from the most trivial to the most sacred. You could say religion, at its most profound, is about that. Even the etymology of the word religion to reattach, is the re-connection between you and God. It is about bridging the spiritual separation between what 'is' and what is not, or what 'is' and what will be, and therefore what 'should be'.

Around the world, people aspire to what should be, trying to make sense of what is happening and inferring what is expected of them. An entity beyond themselves may have the control they don't have. It has intentions about what they should do or be. Priests or spiritual leaders are the medium to explain what is expected and give directions, particularly when a life crisis strikes. When people cannot bear that tension between what 'is' and what 'should be', they may, as a last resort, become suicidal and want to end the tension and return to a state of complete relaxation and nothingness.

Fortunately, life is energy and tension, at the right level.

The angst of being unclear about what we should be or should do is pervasive. In our society, people who have ambitions lead others. They know what others should do. And followers, who feel the pressure of not knowing, are quite relieved to be told what they should do. If people accept that they are lost, they are relieved if someone takes the lead.

If people don't accept what they don't understand, they react in an irrational manner. They know they are lost and need a therapist to guide them, and at the same time, they still do not accept that they don't understand. They argue and tense.

Throughout history, older generations liked to tell younger generations what they should do. Younger generations responded by not wanting to be told what they should do. People tend to do the opposite in reaction to something that dominates them.

Any judgement, such as good, bad, better, worse, or to know that something is beautiful or cold or strange implies a comparison with a norm.

You can be totally in is, and then you are present, aware, in the flow. There is nothing wrong. It is what most spiritual writers describe and promote. Whether it is the Power of Now by Eckhart Tolle or the Buddhist teachings of the Dalai Lama, you don't have to be enlightened to be present. You can be present when you are totally enthralled by a scenery, a book, a symphony, or a dance. 'Is' and 'should be' are on a continuum. If you are at the other end of the scale, in the 'should be', you are frustrated and vibrating with manic energy.

I love being in Africa on safari. Although it is nice to be in the wilderness and see lions, giraffes, and elephants in their natural environment, what I appreciate most is to switch off thinking. There is no judgement, assessment, evaluation, prediction, no should mode. It is just being like the animals, dealing with reality. A hippopotamus is coming out of the river, don't get in its way. A buffalo is spotted, let's do a big loop (if you are on foot). If we don't see animals, it doesn't matter. Just being there is enough. When I talk to people with similar experiences of being in nature, they all say that they feel very present, part of the place around them, they belong. There is no 'should be', it is completely 'is'.

Any judgement, such as good, bad, better, worse, or to know that something is beautiful or cold or strange implies a comparison with a norm.

Think of something that is wrong. That makes you react. It could be in your life, society, or the news. Something like: so and so does this, says that, he is an idiot.

Notice the comparison between what 'is' and what 'should be'. Then notice how your judgment leads the search for evidence to back itself up. Like once you have decided he is an idiot, you find more evidence to confirm the fact.

Try it for yourself. Pick an example of something that should not be.

Map and territory

Have you ever been riveted on an idea and continued when it was not working? You followed the plan, regardless. You followed the map, rather than the territory.

When GPS came out, many stories emerged of people who blindly followed the voice's instructions. They drove into rivers, got their delivery truck stuck in narrow streets, or drove to a place in Russia instead of the one in Germany with the same name (friends of mine did that). They didn't check the territory. They continued because they should.

So what is should? Should is the content of the map. It may have come from your own experience, the lessons and facts you have learnt throughout life. Things happen, we learn and make rules and directives. It becomes our guide for life.

Not only do we learn them ourselves, we also learn from others. It may have been inherited from your culture or your family. Everything you hear through conversations, what you see on TV, and what you read in the newspapers or books forms your map. It may stem from the territory, but it comes to reside in the kingdom of ideas.

Here is an example of a problem between the map and the territory: when speaking English, the French use the French way of enunciating and speaking. Yet, with the exception of the letter o, all other vowels are pronounced differently in English. A speaker learns his native language orally by hearing words long before seeing them written. On the other hand, French pupils learning English see it written and cannot help saying it as a French person would read it. They apply their rules, how the words should be pronounced, the way they know to be the right way. I know French people who have lived in England for many years and still pronounce English words the French way, despite having heard them correctly spoken by native English people. This is because they operate from their map rather than being in the territory.

The territory is what you experience. It is embodied; you think with all of you, brain, mind, body, soul. It is in the present, in the physical reality.

Experience is based on reality. Everybody knows that sex can be explained or described, formally or informally, illustrated with the use of pornography or school educational material, but that would never match the reality of it. We know it's not the same thing.

The two systems, one which conceptualises, and the other perceiving experiences based on reality, are very different and often confused. People talk about other's experience as if they understood. Politicians get criticized because they are detached from reality yet want to dictate how people should operate. When people tell others what to do, they usually come from their own map. We do it to ourselves. We impose our map of how things should be.

We create our map for the use we are going to make of it. Reality is highly subjective. That is why it is important to distinguish facts from fiction as much as you can. Subjectivity tends to see everything as fact.

You may have got stuck trying to understand why something happened. Most clients do. When they are unsuccessful, they come to see a therapist.

Clients have a problem, and they try to figure it out: the way they think it works, looking for causes and effects, what it all means. They create a map for it. The more they try to sort it out, the more they complicate the map. The past, the present, the future, other people, what they are not in control of; it's all in. And yet even though they think about it constantly, it doesn't help. So, it has to be more complicated. There must be some other causes and effects.

In contrast to a complicated worst-case scenario map, we can have a simple one: "Going out on Friday night is great". There is no more detail than that, but it is enough. The map can be simple but sufficient for what we need it for.

The cognitive looks ahead to make decisions. Those decisions logically make sense. By cognitive, I mean think, plan, strategise, predict, etc.

The embodied reality part projects itself in the future and has concerns. The body is also a body of knowledge. If you, the cognitive part, are looking ahead and think, "I can do that," but you are missing some information, the body will produce anxiety. It's being asked to be put into a future scenario where it senses danger and asked to make a decision or take action. That conflict is a functional conflict.

When the map is incomplete, we fill the gaps based on what we know and have experienced in the past. The unknown often generates anxiety, so we fill in the gaps with made-up content, sometimes worst-case scenarios, and pessimistic projections. We have to be cautious, so we feel scared. Something negative is always better for the brain than something unknown.

The reality of what really happens is in the territory, here and now. The problem is how people perform it, how they describe it, and what they put the emphasis on. The more effort focusing on the map, the more it takes them away from the territory.

People who worry about the future are in the map, not in the territory. People who talk about other people's problems are in the map, not the territory. It is not that people should not be in the map. It is necessary to be in the map to plan ahead. The problem is that the two are mixed up. We need both, but we need to be clear that they are not the same. It is the relationship between the two that matters.

To be efficient in any physical discipline, you have to stop thinking and let the body make it happen. It is based on experience. Riding a bicycle, swimming, walking, hitting a ball with a racket, or with your hands, hitting a nail with a hammer, or typing on a keyboard; are all based on experience. Even forms of thinking activities, such as speaking, counting, and imagining, are not based on deliberate conscious effort but on what the brain can do mindlessly.

Often, we are not cognisant of what is happening because we have not reached a threshold that makes us register what is happening. People don't realise the effects of sugar and alcohol because they are only aware of the pleasure in the moment. They don't realise the effects they would have on them through time. They don't see the result ten years later when their liver can't cope, and they have man boobs and a beer belly. People don't see it happening. So, they don't have a choice. To be aware, they would need to be external and see the difference today and in ten years side by side, like they would see two pictures with differences. To regulate a behaviour within the system, they need to have the risks increasing and hit a threshold of non-acceptable. In the territory, this awareness comes naturally from the constraints within the system. For example, animals would not gorge to the point that they are unable to run away from danger. Or when they do because they know winter is coming and they need to stack up reserves. They know that intrinsically, through instinct or experience. That's not the map; it is the territory.

Psychology students may have spent five years studying all the theories of the different approaches, but they just have a map, a very sophisticated map. They are petrified of being in the territory and seeing a real client. That reliance on the map, when not balanced with experience of the territory, is detrimental. It gives them a false sense of security that would be tested in real life. So some may prefer to stay in the map. They do experiments and research; it is safer.

In general, people can understand the theory, but it doesn't mean they have assimilated it through real experience. I encounter that when I discuss concepts with my colleague Kieron. He explains his ideas. I understand them conceptually, but not in a way that makes a connection with what is already there in my model of reality. I am very aware I only have a conceptual understanding of what he says, only an intellectual experience.

Similarly, for clients, they get advice, but if it is not already in their experience, it is just a detached concept. Again, it makes sense; but it is not applicable to them.

Take Leadership, a much talked about subject. It is often about theories and ideas. Many leaders love being surrounded by advisors and telling others what to do. It breeds a culture of consultants. They all create maps about how people who are already doing a job should do it. Whereas real leadership happens organically.

Many people are using their brains in an office context, strategising, making plans, thinking of conjectures that may happen in the future, and stressing. They are in a virtual world, others' map most of the time. It is disconnected from reality. At the weekend, they love going to the countryside, their garden, or a park to reconnect to nature. Nature is the territory. Having spent so much of their energy on the map, an abstraction of the territory, people crave that time spent in a reality where they feel connected. It is vital for their health.

A good example of map and territory, or between should and is, is knowing that the people around you will die. You know it as a concept. It is in the map. When you have a very sick relative, you are prepared for what will happen. Although the map and the reality are getting closer, it doesn't make it easier when it becomes a reality. When you lose someone dear, you really experience that they are not the same.

The concept map and territory is not mine. I know it to be attributed to the scientist Alfred Korzybski, although it is clear that many thinkers throughout history would have thought of the distinction.

Many artists and thinkers have illustrated it in their own way, such as Rene Magritte, who painted a pipe, with the comment in the painting "Ceci n'est pas une pipe" (this is not a pipe). He meant that the picture of a pipe is not a pipe.

> If you are in the street, look around you. Now, take your smartphone, and look at the map of where you are. Notice they are not the same. Notice that the map is an abstraction of reality. If you want to go somewhere, you need both. The map what is in between your hands, or in your head; and moving in the territory.
>
> If you look at a map of where you are and where you want to go, let say from the post office to the bakery, you need to make sense of it on the map, the route, then you have to raise your head and look at where you are, make a connection with your departing point, the post office, and then figure out the direction you have to take, right, left, straight ahead or turn around.
>
> You need to have a representation of the map in the territory. It is obvious that the two are different. One is an abstraction, the

other is a reality. You have to make a transition, a translation between one system and the other.

Now take someone you admire or pity. Realise that what you know about them is a map.

You could try to walk in their shoes, be empathetic, but it is still not the territory. Even if you were to literally try their shoes, you would still not have the same experience they have when they wear them!

What is happening between 'is' and 'should be'?

It could be a happy surprise, as in something you were not expecting is better than what you had expected, but in the context of this book on regaining control, most of our efforts are about reducing the unwanted tension between the two.

We are mostly between now and next, between what 'is' and what 'should be' or could be. The less tension between the two, the more you can be present. If, on an ongoing basis, there is no difference, you may even be enlightened! In total constant acceptance of what is. I would assume you are not.

So, what is the relationship between 'is' and 'should be'? How is it experienced?

Think back to a situation when you didn't understand what someone was telling you or trying to follow the instructions on an Ikea flat pack. You probably felt frustrated when you did not understand. You were frustrated because you should understand, and didn't. It needs to make sense.

That tension dominates the thinking in many ways. It is what prevents people from being in the present. They are not listening when you are speaking and going into their own train of thought instead, especially when they are under pressure and overwhelmed. Like a boss giving instructions to an employee whose mind is elsewhere because he is too concerned about the amount of work they already have and how they won't cope. It is a regular feature with my mum with things to do with technology or explaining Wi-Fi to my sister. It doesn't go in. Between 'is' and 'should be' is a black hole that makes everything disappear; their minds go blank. In fact, it is what magicians use with misdirection. You expect something should happen, and something else happens. If there was no tension between what happened and what should have happened, there would not be magic.

An extreme example that you may have experienced: you sit down and the seat is an inch or a couple of inches lower than expected. Do you remember what you experienced? Your heart jumps into your throat. You experience a moment of terror. It doesn't last because you understand what happened. But at the moment it happens, something should be there, and it isn't. In that split second between the expectation of the seat not being met and your bum touching it is the super-condensed effect of what people experience over many years: the frustration and anxiety of a life unfulfilled.

People can get stuck in ongoing tension because what has happened and what should have happened can't be resolved. I found most depressions stem from an event that should not have happened and not being able to move on from the fact that it has happened. Consequently, people are stuck in blame, guilt, remorse, anger, etc. that develops into depression. Although when people are in the depression itself, there is little tension between 'is' and 'should be'. There is no energy between the two. They are pretty much overlapping. People are then resigned to the way it is.

The psychiatrist Elisabeth Kübler-Ross identified five stages of grief: denial, anger, bargaining, depression, and acceptance. You could say those are the progression of responses to what is happening between what 'is' and what 'should be'.

Clients, and people in general, tell you about their life as a narrative of a series of related events and things that happened that make them unhappy, angry, and chronically frustrated. What we call a narrative is the way you present a story. "this happened and this happened and that meant ...." It puts elements together with a general theme or themes. The story repeated becomes a myth, a presentation of identity. Sharing it gets others' understanding and sympathy, and reinforces it, validates it. It also prevents the person from being open and moving on. 'Is' and 'should be' are intertwined and indissociable. There is no clarity. This happened, and what is implied is peppered with should not have happened, should not be.

A client was reporting what had happened at work. She was upset. Her narrative was about what her colleagues said in a meeting. It was a mixture of facts and interpretations, broken trust, betrayal, and lies, all jumbled together. A judge in a tribunal tries to discern the facts to make sense of the situation. The same process is necessary for anyone to separate facts and fiction to move on.

Pick an example of what 'is' and what 'should be', like what you have accomplished in your life, and what you should have accomplished. Or the email you should have received and have not.

Notice the form that takes the difference, the tension.

It could be frustration or a happy surprise.

Pick another example and another; do that throughout the day. Notice how all your reactions are a response to the difference between what 'is' and what 'should be'.

Regain control of your life

So what?

Whenever someone describes a situation and there is emotion present, they automatically compare it to what 'should be': "He should be there by now", "That chicken is not cooked", and "That's a surprise". It could be a good or bad surprise.

- You want to focus on a piece of work, but it is not happening. You can't concentrate, are constantly distracted, and are always interrupted. You should be able to do your work undisturbed.

- You are instructed to do something. You react against being told. They should recognise that you are capable, not tell you how to do things.

- You want to talk to someone but are aware of protocol, what should or should not be said. You should be able to say it straight.

- You want to do something, but there are constraints, not enough time, and no clear expectations. You should not have that pressure.

- It is not fair. It should be fair.

As covered in the paragraph on foreground/background, you may sense that something is wrong. You are supposed to do something, to remember something. But what is it? You may be wasting your time. You don't know what, but you are unconsciously comparing what 'is' to what 'should be'.

If you consider why you are cranky: you should not be in this boring job; you should make use of your talent; you should be able to trust your partner. But you may not be able to put your finger on it. You cannot identify it. You don't know why, but you are concerned, angry, or anxious. There is something that should be and isn't.

A student who had been dumped by his girlfriend was depressed and could not think about anything else. He was inconsolable. What could he do to reconnect to other aspects of his life, like studying, and put this episode in perspective? I asked him to practise gratitude and focus on the things he enjoyed. He couldn't. Being grateful when he was feeling sorry for himself was not going to work. He was looking in the negative direction, what he had lost. He could not look and appreciate what he had. Not yet. We had to bring what should not have happened to 'it has happened' and work on accepting it first.

You are either going towards where you want to go or away from it. If someone easily feels dominated by the demands they put on themselves, like having to do their homework or a chore, or the demands others make of them are unwanted, they can easily escape in 'away from mode'. Sometimes it is expressed as Attention Deficit Disorder. Their mind wanders. They are not present. Yet, they are capable of being focused on what they find interesting. Some people are very sensitive to this and are less able to control their attention. They can be totally immersed in their activity, regardless of the context, but if there is the slightest sense of domination, they are in avoidance mode.

If you do nothing but stand still, it is also frustrating. You should do something. Doing nothing can't be a solution. Or you need to reframe doing nothing as doing something useful, like having a rest or taking stock.

You can work by yourself or with someone else's help to identify what should be. I am here, and I want to be there. It is now clear. Even how to get there is clear. Your mood has improved, and your attitude is more constructive and optimistic. Your relationship with the world has changed. You are re-energised.

Your mood, attitude, and frame of mind are deeply indicative of the relationship between 'is' and 'should.' People can get resentful when they compare what is in front of them to what they don't have. If they consider someone successful, they judge themselves as not. The other is a symbol, a comparative representation of their failure, or whatever form the judgement takes. They can be jealous and angry when they consider themselves as 'have not' and a successful person in front of them as 'have.' For the rioter who vents their frustration, a person, a shop window, or a car can symbolise what they are angry about.

They would be aware of the anger they feel towards the object of their resentment, but probably not of the unconscious polarised comparison that takes place, what the object represents.

When we get angry and triggered by an external event, we are less likely to pay attention to our own response. We are absorbed, spellbound, by the event. When people argue, as in a couple's dispute, their attention is on finding evidence against the other person. If someone annoys us, the excitatory mode gets us stuck on them, on the external object of our attention.

The energy spent on getting frustrated and fired up on the external event could be better used on resolving the self-management issue so that you can escape the pattern of reactivity to the trigger.

Something you want and enjoy can also be a source of tension and frustration. Have you ever experienced something that you wanted to happen that always seemed to go wrong?

Harry wanted to write a book. He enjoyed writing and had written most of it. Yet he couldn't get himself to finish it. He would write and suddenly stop, unable to realise what was holding him back, like a fly hitting a window, not understanding the obstacle, persisting yet not succeeding.

He had developed a pattern of starting and not finishing, which was a source of frustration. The closer he got to finishing, the closer he got to the unconscious feeling of frustration, and so when he got too close, he would stop. Writing the book gradually became an imperative.

Whenever we conceive an idea, it is connected to the reason. It is alive with a sense of possibility, in an excitatory mode. But later, it has no juice any more. It is disconnected from the environment that gave it life, like an orphan. It can be felt as just an instruction felt as a domination, or a hollow fact. The wanting to write a book is now a mixed bag of frustration, unreciprocated love, and confusion.

So, we got him to develop a dynamic connection to why he was writing the book as he was writing, diverting the frustration of being unsatisfied that he was not there yet, to spur him on. As a result, he now feels enjoyment in having written whatever he writes each day and takes pride in his achievement.

Usually, issues are addressed during the therapy session, and to reinforce the change, clients are supposed to do homework in between sessions. But they don't feel the need to do so any more because they now feel good. Now that it doesn't seem necessary, the homework becomes a domination.

There are two levels. One in which you operate and can access, the other that regulates how you operate and where there are glass ceilings against which you bump.

In that complex system, many comparisons and judgements operate, often in conflict at different levels. On the one hand, you are happy about what you did; on the other hand, you are sad about how it happened and are angry about how it came to be, but you are happy that you took part.

I have a friend who, in his youth, was a real daredevil, an adventurer. He still thinks of himself as able to deal with anything. The reality is that he wanted to move to a new city and yet has not visited the city he wanted to move to. He doesn't know where he will stay, what he will do, or what he needs. Too many unknowns stopped him from ever going with his intentions. He is not in the 'can mode' any more. When he thinks of himself, he remembers himself as he once was. That image of himself has not changed. Yet, with age, his attitude has changed. He is not bold any more but cautious. So he is stuck in a frustrating, depressing state of passivity. You probably know people around you whose self-image is not updated, but to what extent is that the case for you?

Every mature man I have talked to says they know they are no longer attractive to young women, but they are still 25 years old in their minds. So there is a discrepancy between how they see themselves and how they know others see them.

Pick something that made you angry.

Notice that it comes from something that shouldn't be.

Now notice your compulsive fixation with the object of the anger.

Do you find it difficult to maintain a detached awareness that it is simply a difference between what 'is' and what 'should be'?

Additionally, from an exercise in assertiveness from my training days, when you find yourself reacting to an emotional trigger, instead of being accusatory, like telling someone everything that they have done is wrong, you can use a formula. That formula is "when you…, I feel…, because…" as in "when you interrupt me, I feel angry, because I feel like you don't care about what I have to say." instead of reacting uncontrollably to an emotional trigger, this simple technique will uncover the reasons that make you upset. You can do this in a journal, not only when someone upsets you, but with life in general, and everything that happens.

Tension in time and space

"If you aren't in the moment, you are either looking forward to uncertainty or back to pain and regret." Jim Carrey

When something is not complete in the past, when something happened that shouldn't have, there is incompletion, and the mind, the ego, is stuck in going back through it, trying to understand and justify how one feels now.

"My grandparents always preferred my older brother. It made me feel lesser. That was unfair. Why? Why did they do that?"

Similarly, one may not be able to be present to here and now because of what will happen in the future. "What am I going to do when my children have left home?"

Being stuck in the past or anxious about the future is a self-induced trance. Nothing else matters. They prevent clients from doing what they need to do, and during sessions they can't help but go back to what happened or what will happen.

People are tense because they are attached to the way it should be. When achievements and success are not met, their endeavours are considered a waste of time. Their thoughts revolve around that frustration.

The difference between is and should, could be in space or time, or with a thing or a resource.

People are annoyed when things are not in their right place. What goes in their physical environment goes in their mind environment. In the mind, things should be ideally aligned or in the right position in relation to each other, at the right distance, and in the right sequence.

For example, some forms of therapy are based on replacing family members where they should be in the geographical map of the participant's mind. They do so by rearranging the group's participants to represent family members in different configurations in the room.

Rearranging priorities and values are equally important. It is effective in order to feel what is right, decide and proceed. When they are not, it creates a conflict of interest or indecision. Ordering the priority of what matters is simple yet powerful.

Even when telling a story, the ordering is important. People always think that before they tell you about this, you need to know about that. They would interrupt you when you talk about your holiday because before that, they should tell you about their experience in that place, or what happened to a familiar friend. Partly in order not to forget but partly because they have it organised in their mind that the story should be in a particular sequence. This now, that then. Not the other way around.

People can get stuck because they think they have to do something before something else. They may be right because there is an external imperative, like something that needs to be done for work, that others are waiting for. But sometimes, it is a constraint that is subjective and doesn't serve them, and it can be difficult to distinguish what is objective and what is subjective. It happens to me, even when writing this book, which took a significant chunk of my time. I would start revising a chapter and lose my concentration. I could not focus. I would feel that I have to do another task, check my emails and reply to the ones that mattered and could come back appeased and refreshed to review the chapter.

A classic question to get people to consider what they would like if they didn't have constraints is, "what would happen if you won 10 million in the lottery?" This gives them a totally different proposition, where the constraints have disappeared, and therefore they can relax and rearrange things in a way that works for them.

For time, the question could be, "if you had all the time in the world…"Everything happens in time. Everyone at various points, in various situations, would like more time. You lost or failed because you didn't have enough time. You are under pressure because you should have more time.

Either behaviour, completing the past, or anticipating the future, is a need to regain some control, but sometimes control can be gained by accepting that it is out of our control.

Stopping worrying about the future can be resolved by building resources, such as planning. And for what happened in the past, it's a matter of accepting and realising that the self-inflicting cost of holding on is not worth it.

> Are you thinking too much about the past or about the future?
>
> Take some time to consider whether you spend time reminiscing about the past, having regrets, or whether you are always trying to control the future, knowing there is nothing you can do about it but worry.

And relax....

We need stimulation and tension – as long as we are in control. What is out of the ordinary, out of the norm, fascinates. When we watch TV, magazines, or social media, things like violence and rudeness, attract viewing because we become alert, aroused, and energised. It is what people want to see on TV: drama. TV gives us a safe distance to experience it without danger. It gives us the safety comfort zone. It is entertaining and captivating, maybe with a hint of fear.

When things are different from the norms, there is an automatic comparison between 'is' and 'should'; it should be like this, and it is like that. It makes you react. It produces tension, like two magnets that repel each other and are also drawn to each other.

That tension is for the two poles to be back together.

You can bring 'is' and 'should' together or intentionally keep them apart. The tension between the two can be harnessed.

In the field of sport, we are bottom of the league and should be top. That frustration can be used for motivational purpose. You may want to keep the two, 'is' and 'should', separate purposefully. You may want the polarity. People put pictures of things they aspire to on their walls or desks to motivate themselves. Teams have monthly sales targets they have to reach for the end of the month. Goals empower because you are not where you should be and you can get there. You can feel that tension as a positive motive for action.

The danger of bringing the two together and dissipating the tension can result in making you passive. There is no energy for wanting to close the gap, like when people are depressed, or resigned to their condition, or satisfied. When that energy is low and static, there is no more incentive to act.

What if you remove the tension that makes you want to do something? Dissatisfaction is what has caused everyone to engage in activities to progress. It's motivation. Humanity would still be like monkeys without it.

Additionally, we could consider the meaning of 'should,' from 'should' that is not going to happen, to 'should' that could happen. The first one is like, "I should but don't have to," whereas the second one is more like, "I have to, it's a must". It is more like an external imperative. Along that continuum is a progressive increase of the pressure and domination of the 'should'. It becomes more external and dictating. "I should go out" (but I am feeling lazy). "I should go out" (because there is an imminent danger in staying in). The intensity of the 'should' can go from trivial to essential.

We can deliberately change the intensity and probability of the should we deal with. You can imagine that you have a knob and turn that intensity. It is the internal subjectivity, the management of the experience. We can also use questioning and reframing for the same purpose. How can you relieve the pressure, the domination; who says you should? Where does the pressure come from? What will happen if you consider the directive? What if you see the should not as an order but as advice?

The writer and hypnotherapist Stephen Gilligan specialises in self-relation. He describes the use of humour, tenderness, and fierceness in the change process. Humour and love are good practices to provoke a release of tension. That is why we like comedy. Because of the different meanings given by changing the habitual context, creating tension and releasing it. It feels good releasing tension. It is the rhythm of life. It is what sex is all about. Before we release it, we need to create it.

Even though 'being right' keeps you tense, you can nevertheless practise releasing the tension of the should, not because of letting go of your reasons to be right, but because it is a good and useful practice to relax the tension of the should. In other words, you can be right but relaxed about it. You have to take life seriously to be stressed. It doesn't mean that the situation is not serious, but if you can see the humorous side of things, you relax.

Love also releases tension. A parent trying to calm their crying child would hug them. Being loved helps them to relax. You can do it to yourself by having self-compassion.

Is the 'should' fixed, rigid or negotiable and flexible? Pick an example.

Practise taking a 'should' that has some tension to it and practise lessening the intensity. You can always come back to the rightness of it afterwards.

Now take a should that has little intensity, one that has a flavour of 'eventually' and increase the intensity.

Both are useful exercises to reduce or increase the intensity of the should, so that you regain some control.

Balance

We rest because we have to. Without sleep, we would be stimulated all the time.

Rest is necessary to reset a state that is stressed. Both the body and the mind need to rest, not just to eliminate the stress and fatigue of the day; it also re-energises you for the next day. However, sometimes it is not enough. That is when you want a good holiday, to rest and eliminate the stress but also take some distance from your obligations and come back with the energy to tackle your current situation.

A holiday, in contrast to everyday life, is self-contained, time limited, and away from the environment that causes pressure. It does not observe the same rules as your normal life. You can enjoy yourself relaxing, releasing tension, without stress even if it is an active holiday.

What's different in normal life is the expectations of where I should be. It means having achieved something. Generally, when some people think of normal life: work, demands, deadlines, there is the relentless pressure of expectations. They usually don't have those on holiday. You can forget all of that when you are on holiday, all the expectations of achievement. You can release the tension and relax. We need a holiday, and until the holiday, we have the weekend.

And don't people look forward to weekends! And until the weekend, we have the end of the day.

That is why it is crucial that a healthy life is about maintaining a balance of work, rest, and play. You may know that you are out of balance. Maybe you need more rest or play, or maybe more investment in your work to know that you can enjoy your rest and play, like when exercising.

Often clients don't have what I call punctuation in their life. No commas, full stops, new paragraphs, or new chapters. They need to look at how to add punctuation to make sense of what is happening and stop the ceaseless demands, particularly if they are chronically worrying or depressed. During the session, they take a break from real life. It is a treat. So, they are more flexible. But when they go back to real life, between sessions, they can become tense and stressed again.

Review your life in terms of work, rest, and play.

Think of the quality and quantity of each.

How is the balance, and what could you do to regain some balance?

Acceptance

The longer a situation has lasted, or the more traumatic, the more people would hold on to it. It is difficult to let go.

The story of how to catch the monkey comes to mind. It goes like this: in Indonesia, when the hunters want to catch a monkey, they make a hole in a coconut large enough for a monkey to insert its hand. They put nuts in the coconut. The inquisitive monkey finds the coconut and, grabs the nuts, but now its hand is a fist that is too big to take out of the hole. The monkey does not want to let go of the nuts. It is then easy for hunters to catch the monkey as it can't climb up a tree or swiftly run away. This analogy is useful for many aspects of life when we are stuck because of our attachment to something. For more details about attachment, you can read about Buddhism. The main lesson of the Buddha is that suffering comes from attachment.

The more we have struggled to get those nuts, the more we have invested in getting them, the more we value them, the less we are likely to let go.

When we have maintained a stressful situation for a long time, or we are really upset about something that happened, it creates trauma. The stronger our hold on it, the less likely we want to let go. The ego is inflated and bitter.

Even if the cause of the tension is gone, the tension remains through habit. So that tension becomes the reason to be tense. In the same way that when you have intense physical exercise, you still have the adrenaline in your body, even when it is finished.

I could talk about most of my clients, but I will refer to one in particular. As a child, he was moved around and felt acutely that he was not in control of his life. He reacted with anger to the domination of his lack of freedom. As a result, he now works hard. His contained anger fuels his energy. He proves to his clients and organisation that he is reliable and works long hours. He would leave home at 6 am and return at 9 or 10 pm. He is always under pressure. He responds to tension with more work, like people who fight fire with fire and burn the candle at both ends. It took a while to get him to release the tension of the habit. He has high expectations of himself. The people who know him know him as reliable, hardworking, and always resourceful.

He is the result of a well-constructed systemic vicious circle of his own making.

It's not easy to relax the body. It's not easy to release the tension of the mind either. It's not easy to change the habit of being oneself.

Getting people to let go of their attachment to the situation is not easy. In order to stop being stuck, they have to let go of the tension. They are in a reactive state. They have no choice in the matter and react to tension with more tension. They have everything invested in the reality of the situation. Their mind says it is justified. Their body tension is the context in which they think. So they don't want and can't let go of the nuts.

To let go requires detachment. We normally experience the demand as external, imposed on us. When we can accept it as part of the experience, we can start to let go.

When we change our perspective and learn to consider things globally, systemically, from multiple points of view, we react less against being dominated. We are more detached. The tension between this and that diminishes, and we are more able to let go.

Time usually helps to relieve tension. It's a bit like how tiredness gets us to fall asleep and releases the tensions of the day. The exception is when we are chronically exhausted and can't even rest in our sleep. Similarly, someone who is so angry or depressed can't let go. It's like a cramp. Even if we wanted to let go of the tension, we couldn't. It's chronic tension.

Here is a speech I had written: Story of the fear of the lion

> Thinking about the situation, my mind is constantly refocusing, like a camera, struggling to focus on one thing and not being able to stay with it. My mind is conflicted. I can't settle on one position. It was already scary to see the lions from the jeep at such a short distance. Now it is about being on foot in the wilderness.
>
> Before I describe the struggle of my mind, I have to add that it is unbearably hot in Africa in the dry season.
>
> The guide proposes taking us to a pride of lions, maybe 20 of them, first thing in the morning, where they are probably going to be in an amphitheatre. We are going to walk right into the middle of them. Those are not animals who are used to humans. We are in a remote and wild part of Zimbabwe. The idea is that if the lions are happy, it is fine. If they are not, we would walk back. Simple. Simple?
>
> Although I slept like a log, others have heard the lions very nearby last night. So nearby, in fact, that the first thing we found as we leave the camp is a pair of shorts from a staff member. Someone, something, took them from the laundry line and took them off to tear them apart. If that is not a premonitory sign…

As the guide takes my friend and I down the path, following the paw prints of the lioness, the culprit of the prank, here is what is going on in my mind.

My logical mind is thinking, right: context, this is a guided search. The guide is knowledgeable and experienced.

The lions want to avoid us. If you don't run, turn your back, or are down, they don't think you are prey. If you don't react, they would avoid you because you don't fit the pattern of a prey, which runs when they see the lion. Well, that's what I have been told.

Except, one guy was killed by a lion whilst he was taking his shower. I later saw the plaque on the tree where he camped and was killed. First, the shorts in the laundry, and now someone killed because they washed. Basically, lions react badly to cleanliness.

Put simply, the attitude of guides and my friend is that if you don't do anything that annoys the animals, they are fine. My friend Marc is not scared. He has come here to Africa doing those trips several times. So, my logical mind tries to say, it is alright. That's the industry. The animals want to avoid us, we avoid confrontation too. Each of us are quite happy to walk away.

Meanwhile, I am going along because I don't want to be a party pooper. And I don't want to show I am scared.

But despite thousands of years of evolution, I am still a monkey and feel like one. Monkeys fear lions.

My brain tells me it's a bad idea. My guts tell me it's a bad idea.

I am not equipped to face a lion. I can't fight. I can't outrun.

Just the sight of those big monsters when they look at you, stand up, and walk towards you fills me with anguish.

I don't belong to this context. And I know I have no control over what could be happening, and I am supposed to have the control of not running and staying calm. Well, it is not the case. I am anxious, and the more I rationalise, the more the monkey mind is going crazy.

Today I am trying to convince myself that I belong to the context of safari, tracking animals, and big cats. That it is not dangerous; otherwise, they would not do it. Our guide, Mark, is sensible and says he wants to return to his family. So, if I take a global perspective of the system, myself the monkey I have to reassure, the lion's perspective and the context of the guided walking safari, then it is just being part of the system. And because I am a psychotherapist, added to the mix is a fascination in observing the turmoil within.

We didn't go to the lion amphitheatre in the morning because it was raining hard.

Somehow, I relaxed and got accustomed to the idea that it was normal. We moved to another camp; as we arrive, several cars are there looking for a lion. It has been sighted. We are the only ones to get out of the vehicle. People in their cars look at us as we disappear into the bushes as if we are crazy. I am the first one to see it—a dark mane lion. And I am excited but not afraid of it, as a child would be. It seems surprised to see me. He stares for a moment, turns around, and walks deeper into the bushes. Soon it disappears.

I feel very proud. I have faced my first lion. I live to tell the tale.

Regain control of your life

Think of a situation in your life charged with emotion, fear or anger. It's not difficult to think of it from your perspective. That is what you usually do. Now try to see it from the object of your anger or fear's perspective. And now think of it globally, as a system. Notice the emotion diminishes. If you repeat this exercise, eventually, the emotion will reduce to the point where you can accept what happened/will happen objectively without it being a big deal.

The gearbox model

When someone needs to do something, like talking to someone where they fear it may escalate into an argument, they become anxious. Firstly, what to say and how to say it creates anxiety because it implies possibilities that things could go wrong. Secondly, they are pushing themselves to do something they don't want to do. That's another source of anxiety. It's like if somebody wanted to push you into a swimming pool, but you don't know how to swim, or pushing yourself to do it, because you are embarrassed that you cannot do what others can. The more you push yourself, the more you would have reluctance and resistance. That stubborn little donkey in you has wisdom.

In positive psychology and coaching, when people talk about what they don't like, they are usually asked, "what would you like instead?" Most of the time, it annoys them. They know what they don't want but don't know what they want. The question frustrates them. They can't figure out what they want, as it requires being in a creative, relaxed mode, and they are going in the opposite direction, avoiding what they don't want, which is a tense mode. The coach who asks them what they want is, unknowingly, in a positive mindset, so it is easy for them to propose that, they don't have the same pressure. The discrepancy between operating modes adds to the client's annoyance and frustration.

People know they are tense and in problem mode. They know they should calm down and release the tension, but they are in a paradox. Relaxing becomes a domination, something they should do. Therefore, they react and rebel against the command, especially if it is external, instructed by someone else, or if they have a particularly reactive personality. "Don't tell me to relax!" They are stuck in tension.

What can you do? The first thing is to recognise that you have to stop pushing yourself before you can confront what you fear. You have to see it as a matter of fact, otherwise the tension continues because you don't accept.

For example, many people postpone to the last moment doing their tax return. Imagine you are one of them. You can substitute tax return for whatever task you find yourself procrastinating. Stop for a moment and admit to yourself, without guilt or shame, that you are postponing your tax return.

We can analyse the situation better if we don't put that pressure on ourselves.

How can you do that?

Sometimes people are so attached to their anger that they are out of control. The sense of righteousness is very connected to the sense of who they are. It is them against the situation. It's personal. Their whole being is at stake, not just the issue. But even if they want to calm down, it may be difficult not to feel that they have given in.It is particularly noticeable in couple therapy. Despite their best intentions, it is very difficult for partners not to justify themselves, pointing to their efforts and how the other is not responding as they should. It is tough not to criticise, not to make the other one wrong and make themselves right. Although when they are venting their frustration, there are periods when they would calm down and can accept that there is a cost in continuing this way.

But, if we can put aside the sense of injustice and just deal with reality and accept it, we can regain some control. We can accept what we can and acknowledge what we cannot accept. That in itself releases tension. Starting by accepting what we can change sets the direction for the mind.

It is difficult to move on when we have to acknowledge and accept reality whilst we are angry or frustrated. I describe it to clients as if they are driving a car in the wrong gear. They are struggling, stumbling, and funny hopping. They must admit to themselves that they have to do something before engaging with a solution: they have to use the clutch and go into neutral before going into the right gear.

I broke down the process of acceptance into four stages. Each has its relevance:

1. Acknowledge the tension
2. Agree that it is not working, that you are stuck
3. Accept to let go
4. Act, decide

You may find that momentarily you accept to let go, but the reactive process starts again, or an aspect is not accepted, and you come back to vent your anger. Then, you just have to accept again. It is like physical exercise. To become flexible, you have to stretch repetitively over a period of time.

Focus on what prevents you from accepting and start the same process of acknowledging and accepting that aspect. Within that aspect, what can you accept? And what can you just acknowledge?

Agreeing gives way to deciding because when you decide, you break the tension. It's a turnaround. You have a course of action and regain control, which is ultimately what you want to do in any situation.

Whereas the mind usually flip-flops between 'this but that' and bickers, which causes and maintains tension, the practice of acknowledging, agreeing, and accepting is grounded in a somatic experience, releasing tension.

You will find that when you start resolving the first issue, then the second, and the third, you don't have to address them all because your mind is now primed to resolve issues as they arise. You are again resourceful, ready to move on, and ready to tackle problems. Until next time, and you have to start the same process again.

What happens is that you know that you have to accept. You know this cognitively, but the somatic mind, i.e. the body, experiences it as being told what to do and being dominated. So, you have to accept that you feel dominated. And having to accept that makes you feel that it is not right. But you have to accept that in order to relax. As such, the mind alternates between accepting, being dominated, accepting, and being dominated. Until it stops.

An example is forgiveness. We often know that we should forgive, but we keep returning to what happened. We can't let go. The sense of injustice keeps us focussing on what should be. Eventually, we cool down and know we need to forgive, that there is a cost in remaining righteous. However, a reminder of what happened goes through our minds, and we get angry again. We know we have to accept what happened, accept that we get worked up, and accept that it is OK. It takes time to accept, like a horse accepting being ridden.

Everybody knows you can't help someone who has not asked for it. People know that it is intrinsically true for themselves too. Somebody has to want to change. Clients who see a therapist have naturally gone through the gearbox model. They have already recognised that they have a problem, realised that their solution is not working, decided to do something about it, and acted. They make an appointment.

Any situation where you don't know how to do a task, don't have the knowledge or the information and feel under pressure to do something; you are better off without the pressure to do whatever it is you are to do.

Acknowledge that you have the pressure. Accept that it doesn't help. Agree it would be better without, and decide what you want to do. Once you have decided, you have removed the uncertainty. You have let go of the tension. You can operate normally until the next tension. Once again, change gear. Acknowledge, agree, accept, and act.

If what you do is not working, call the AAAA. (Acknowledge, Agree, Accept, Act.)

First, you can start applying this acceptance process to external things, like what is happening around you. Then, as you practise the muscle of acceptance, you will start to accept your responses to situations. For example, you may get angry at the way people behave on public transport. Anger puts your attention outside. "Why don't they move out of the way! They should let people come out before they come in! What world do I live in!?" You tense your mind and body. Your senses will be automatically external, noticing everything they do that is wrong.

Your response will be anger. Maybe later, when the anger subsides, you release tension, and you may experience sadness. Maybe through compassion, you understand the other person's perspective and make room for the reasons for their behaviour. As you start to accept others, you release more of the tension. As you release the tension with the external world, you can become aware of the tension in your internal world. You can become aware of your internal dialogue. Up until now, your attention may have been compelled to notice outside. The way you judge people. The tension in your body is maybe not so much about them and what they should not do as it is about your own self-management. You can start to question and become aware of not agreeing with the aggressiveness you display. You may start finding it unacceptable and decide you don't want to react like this any more. And then through being disappointed when you do and proud when you don't, in other words, through negative and positive reinforcement, you can control your outbursts.

This whole chapter describes the process of being able to let go, of accepting.

Your task, if you accept it, is to practise this process.

Pick examples you can practise.

If you are reluctant to do it, use this as your first example!

Many clients have been carrying a card with them with a reminder:

1 Acknowledge the tension

2 Agree that it is not working

3 Accept to let go

4 Act, decide what you want

You could do the same.

An important detail

Most people would report feeling alone when they are worried and under pressure. You can verify it for yourself. Try to worry now. Pick an example.

You probably feel like a child on their own, alone. You are being passive and helpless.

To regain some control and start being active, you need to have a relationship with yourself. For example, it can be being able to reassure yourself and having compassion for yourself. This is subtle but easily overseen. It is the first step in what makes everything work. It is so easy to overlook the importance of this. It is simple yet crucial.

When you are worried or anxious, you are overwhelmed. Despite the visceral grip of the feeling, you need to regain some control by starting a dialogue with yourself and being heard. Even by saying something like, "I am feeling bad. I think something could go wrong."

In the absence of someone else to reassure and comfort you, you need to do it for yourself: "It's OK to feel bad."

When you start talking and reassuring yourself, you lower the demand and increase your resource. Anything positive you would say would increase your resource. "It's OK to feel bad.", "Everybody would feel bad in this situation." "You have felt bad before, and nothing bad actually happened." "If something goes wrong, you will say so. People would understand that things happen."

Habituation

In addition to the gear box model, there is another way of accepting what you think 'should not be'.

Take stock of what is happening. Have a sense of yourself and your space. When you have settled, think of something that annoys you, angers you or that you find difficult to accept. The important thing here to remember is that it is not about changing anything but about being in a better state to deal with the issue. Instead of pushing yourself to accept, which would create tension and reluctance, you are going to stay in your space and pull the object that you need to accept towards you, until you don't react in an angry way.

Remember by object we mean an idea, a proposition, a suggestion, a belief.

Work on your state first. Be relaxed, serene, in an acceptance mode. Work on getting into that state. Then think of the object of your frustration, anger or incomprehension. Bring the object into your space very slowly. If you start to react, move the object back a bit, until you are ready to start again. Get it in your space until you are no longer react. Through habituation, the emotional charge discharges. That way, you are not being constrained, but in control.

This process of habituation happens naturally over time. It does happen naturally with losses. Over time we get habituated to the loss.

Becoming creative

As you let go of the tension, you can become more creative. Creativity in this context means being free of constraints. When you are free of constraints, you are free of automatic responses and can create rather than react. It doesn't happen at the click of your fingers. It is a gradual improvement in your life; like for a dog to stop automatically barking at anything. It would take positive reinforcement for the automatic behaviour to be replaced by a controlled response.

You can suspend the constraints of everyday life for a moment, as when you would say, "Imagine that you have won the lottery. What would you do?"

Whilst you consider this proposition, the constraints of your current situation would dissipate but would eventually return when you come back to reality: "Yes, but I haven't won the lottery." However, that little glimpse into what is possible may give you enough traction for moving forward. In that window, you would have let go of your restrictive hold on reality. It would have the same effect as the gearbox model.

With less stress, you are more able to be with and appreciate what is. You can deal with what is, rather than perceived threats that don't yet exist. In a tense state, the external world becomes a threat because you cannot cope. You can't take any more, only protect yourself from demands. But when the energy is not spent on defending oneself, it is available for creation.

Tara, a client, personified her internal anxiety as the 'gremlin'. We did not try to get rid of it but instead sought to not let it rule her. So she chose to leave it at home when she went out. She could now negotiate and say to it, "I am busy now. I will deal with you later". That changed the balance of power and control and therefore her relationship to her anxiety.

The beginning of creation is small steps and feedback. It starts with the feeling that something you have presented to yourself is good. The energy this appreciation generates is directed towards more generation of ideas that you can externalise to the world, as a thought, a sound, a movement.

Being in creative mode means you can start from anywhere. Most of the time, we are stuck because we think we have to start from a given point or follow a sequence. It does not have to be from a particular point, in a particular sequence. Steve, a sculptor, said he purposefully starts deliberately from what he expects to be wrong so that he doesn't have the pressure of having to be right from the start. He can bounce from that point and rectify it. Being wrong is part of the process to revise and improve. Knowing that you can be wrong and you don't have to be right precludes tension. Or at least the tension that exists is a useful tension rather than an unwanted one. It supports rather than inhibits action.

This is particularly useful for something like writer's block but equally valid for any task that you don't start because you don't know where to start.

Think of a task, what is involved, and start from any point.

If you find yourself resisting starting from any point, ask yourself why you couldn't.

If your task was to write the dictionary, you don't have to start at A. Start from whatever letter takes your fancy.

Stuck and can't move on

Sometimes people can't move on from a relationship. Until someone or something replaces the last one, there is a vacuum. The last person or thing is the reference for what satisfied their needs. Because there is nothing else, the mind goes into a loop back to the previous partner. The mind compares what is there to what is no longer there. The absence is not right, so they come back to it. They are unable to escape the gravity of that relationship. Most people would say they can't help but think of their previous partner because they are still in love. It may have nothing to do with love but with how the mind works and the automatic response to the satisfaction of needs (but clients insist it's about missing their loved one and can't move on).

A dynamic of comparison operates each time people meet a potential new partner. The anxiety, caused by not being in a relationship, creates tension that needs to be resolved by thinking of the previous partner. To dissolve the anxiety of uncertainty, they can create faith that they would eventually meet someone ideal and can start designing them. They have to create a new model, an ideal one with as much detail as possible. If it is too vague, it won't hold in comparison to the old one when they meet a potential partner. Because if there is not a tangible standard, or a list of qualities that can be ticked off in the person's mind, by default they would revert to feeling heartbroken.

What goes for a personal relationship goes for any other kind of relationship. You can use the same principle for a job, a house, or a place, in which you compare old and new.

This does not mean that you have to forget or disown something or someone dear to you. It means if you want to move on, there is a way.

Think of an area in your life where you want to move on.

Notice whether you are stuck because you keep projecting a feeling of longing.

Could you instead create a model of what you would like to have?

Think of its qualities and attributes.

Notice the shift in you when you go from the feeling of longing to the thinking forward to what you want.

Outside of your control

People are stressing themselves by trying to resolve what they have no control over. It's widespread. They get frustrated with something they think they should be able to sort out and can't. It is mostly fuelled by blaming themselves. They can't and they should be able to.

Veronique was trying to figure out why her video camera was not connecting to the TV. She did not know she didn't have the right cable. It could not have worked. She tried to figure it out, but got frustrated, angry, and stressed. Instead of asking someone who knew, she tried to deal with it as if the solution would come to her by some kind of divine intervention.

As we have seen in a previous chapter, everything happens within a frame of meaning. When you change the frame, you change reality. For example, a fear of heights is passive but can be reframed as a fear of falling. It makes a big difference. With a fear of falling, you can become active. You can take precautions. There are two aspects. One is there is nothing you can do if you fall. That is terrifying. Therefore, it causes great anxiety. The other aspect is being active instead of passive. Being able to do something about it, like taking precautions to prevent falling. You do this in this example by finding a safe distance between you and the edge, and being capable of making adjustments. Hence focussing on being in control rather than not in control.

Anxiety in life is much the same. You focus on what could go wrong, and as we have seen, it is even worse if you are unclear about what's happening. You become passive and overwhelmed. You are out of control, on a slippery slope.

Here is a story that seems very popular nowadays:

"One evening, an Indian elder was telling his grandson about the inner turmoil people continually face. He told of a battle between the two wolves inside us all. The first characterised by anger, greed, envy, superiority, and ego; and the second by joy, happiness, kindness, and hope. The grandson pondered on this thought and asked, 'Which wolf wins?'. The grandfather replied, 'the one that you feed' ".

The mind works in a more complex way than in the story, because in reality there is no absolutely good wolf and bad wolf, rather the interaction of complex systems. But the principle is still relevant. It's which one you feed that will be the strongest and will win, the passive/reactive, or active/creative.

Playing a game reduces the scope of what we focus on. It removes anxiety. Players are active and in control of what they are doing. It is addictive because players prefer to stay in that reality, rather than the one where they are unsure and unclear of what to do and feel bad. It is the power of the 'can mode'.

People were divided about Brexit, thinking that others that held differing views were wrong. Yet the complexity of it is so incomprehensible that it is impossible to have a clear, objective opinion about it. You can't possibly comprehend all the aspects and implications of the whole thing. You can have an opinion, or opinions. You can comment. You can take a perspective and speculate. But it is only that; speculation. That is not denying that you are frustrated and exasperated, but it is futile. Better to accept that you are out of your depth because it is too complex. Instead, people have an opinion on which way to go and they defend it because it is their opinion. It belongs to them. Their opinion is them. Their opinion owns them. Yet they feel they have some control. An opinion gives them something stable to hang on to.

Clients ask why they are stuck in the past. Why do they keep thinking about what happened? When they do, they are tense. If they are tense, that must mean there is danger. Where have you faced past danger but from experience?

You can rationalise the past, to put things in perspective. Most psychodynamic therapies work on the principle that if you had the resources you needed when you were a child, you would have had a different experience, and therefore you would be better prepared to address the situation now. That works on the principle that people accept this 'as if scenario'. But sooner or later, the harsh reality of life brings back the inescapable feeling that you are not able to cope.

For instance, people can do a personal development weekend, and from then on have a more positive attitude; but from what I have observed, they need to continue with the same method for the effect to be sustained. Few maintain it. Most slip back to the how it was before the course. Even if the map has changed, the territory has not.

Why? Because the way you have previously dealt with things in the past is ingrained in you. Your beliefs may have changed; you think differently but haven't organically developed the skills that would help you to deal with the demand, unless you have put your learning in action. In that case, you would have evolved.

Most workshops and books, including this one, propose a solution to a problem. If you feel convinced the solution is right, you have to put it in practice. Do not leave it as a good idea, as a good map. Build it in the muscle, apply it in the territory. You have to develop the skills. The whole system of your life would need to evolve.

Throughout history, philosophers and wise men and women have advised dealing with what you can control and not with what you can't. A model that I have presented to clients and friends is that of Byron Katie. I like it for its simplicity. She proposes that there are three aspects to a situation when in conflict: your business, the other person's business, and God's business. Yours is to look after your interests, the other person is to look after theirs, and God's or life's or destiny's is to put you in this situation, for you to learn.

It is another way to say just deal with what is in your control, as opposed to trying to resolve an issue where somebody else has a responsibility for things to change, and understanding that the other person also has needs. For example, frustrated parents: their teenager doesn't want to help with household chores. They have a reactive attitude. It is the role of a teenager to deal with their angst and relation to the world. It is life/God/destiny's business to put you two under the same roof. Your business, as a parent, is to look after yourself, and your needs. You are there to express what you want, in a non-ambiguous, assertive way.

The result is that you are free from trying to apportion responsibility to others. You can focus on your responsibilities and doing what is right for you. That way, you have unburdened yourself of what you cannot carry.

Then work on accepting all those aspects. What belongs to self, what belongs to others, what belongs to the context.

A client said she had felt guilty all her life. She said it came from her upbringing. Her parents made her feel guilty. She had been in therapy for years. I asked her to give me a recent example. She said her son had told her, "I want you to love me more, Mummy." She felt guilty that she was not loving her son enough or not as she should. How could she love him more? How would she know what that meant for her son? More time in front of the TV? More cuddles? A toy? She did not know. She did not have the answer. She did not know what it meant for her son when he said he wanted her to love him more because she had not asked him. It ran in a loop without a conclusion, so the guilt continued. The answer is outside of her control. It is the pattern that allowed her guilt to work. The solution was to ask her son about the missing information. She tried it out and ran several examples, and the guilt dissolved in each case. She had felt guilty because she had not asked. She had not asked because she was feeling guilty.

In 10 minutes, we got rid of chronic guilt. Well, habits die hard, and the guilt may still be lurking if surprisingly reignited, but now she knows what to do.

Take a situation that you have no control of.

Break the pattern of total passivity by finding a tiny aspect in which you can exercise some control.

Pay attention to what not having any control means

Notice the difference it makes from having no control at all, and what this contribution to regaining control makes.

Boundaries

The other side of taking on everybody's business is being unable to keep people outside your boundaries.

I counselled a teacher who worked in a rough school, where kids were rude to her. She thought she had nothing to give any more. She was at the end of her tether, sad and drained. She knew that she was deluding herself by saying she was a giver. But that is what people say to justify tolerating a situation. They give themselves the role where they are the good ones in a difficult world.

We approached the issue in terms of boundaries. I pointed to her that being disrespected by the pupils was a violation of her boundaries. If we could shift sadness to anger, it would make her react.

I often purposefully overstep boundaries with clients who present themselves as lacking confidence. They tend to generalise their passivity and believe it is a fait accompli that they are a certain way. Overstepping their boundaries makes them react. The reasons they find it unacceptable can then be exposed, explored, and harnessed. It is not about them any more, it becomes a matter of principles. We react when a principle that we care about is not respected. They then can redefine for themselves what is acceptable and what is not.

All life, plants, animals, and humans test boundaries and establish thresholds and prescriptive rules. How far they can go and what they can do; learning what's right and wrong for survival.

For a child's development, whether they have an authoritative or nurturing parent, whether the world is a friendly place or not, would drive what they can or can't do or be.

I find it easier to read and concentrate at night because I don't have distractions. It is quiet, not only in the environment of my flat but also in the environment of my head. Many people have said the same. During the day, there are lots of real and imagined demands that create tension.

Some people need to have clear separation and order between various aspects of their life: there is between the professional and the personal, friends and romantic interests, the private and the public, and what is serious and what is fun. Other people don't. They are happy to have an ambiguous line between some or all those aspects. Being too controlled and organised feels like a domination. They want to be free and feel better about not having boundaries between those aspects. Whereas for others, especially when stressed, being able to create protective boundaries is vital. It may also be different for where they need to concentrate rather than be creative.

Some people are able to plan and stick to it. They decide and they do it by themselves, like running or meditating. Others prefer the boundaries offered by a yoga class or going to the gym, going to a place that is dedicated to what they want to do and where they can be undisturbed. Either way, they regain control over unwanted demands by setting boundaries and keeping things at bay, so they can focus on what they want and relax.

On one end of the spectrum, some people are totally present in what they do. If they do yoga, they take the state of harmony between mind and body to what they do next in everyday life. They can easily concentrate even when there is a distraction. They do one thing at a time, thoroughly. They can put clear boundaries between themselves and the world's demands, between the areas of their life, between the past, the future, and the present time.

At the other end, there are people who are always on edge, tense, worried, distracted, and on the lookout for what could go wrong. If they start an activity, they worry that there may be something more important or urgent that they should be doing and are not addressing. They are always stressed, lacking control of their life and destiny. Their present is a mixture of undigested past and unpalatable future. They have an endless list of to-dos without being connected to why they do it and not reflecting on what they have done, never getting the satisfaction of their effort. Many people feel they are constantly dominated by life demands.

Making lists is also a good way of having boundaries. Now that it is on paper, to-dos are not flying around like annoying flies.

Cultivating a way of relaxing is very important. When it is practised regularly, it can be done in a 'can mode'. Then we don't have to think about it. It is done automatically. Stress and depression tend to spread and destroy boundaries. Depression swells like fog and envelops everything. As for stress, people come home from work and are unwillingly bringing the stress with them. It sticks to them like a bad smell. So, developing rituals, routines, and symbolic practices that signify the end of something and the beginning of another phase is crucial. It can be taking off the tie, taking a shower, or having a glass of wine. What is important is to consciously reinforce the meaningful aspect of putting a boundary, a closure.

Think of a ritual you have to signify the end of a period.

If you can't find any, it is a great opportunity to make one up and implement it.

You can ask the people around you what rituals or actions they take.

Where else would it be useful?

Plan where it could be implemented, like when going to bed, and what sequence you would put in place.

Regain control of your life

Relationships

If you work in a team environment, you would know that the most important thing to keep harmony and good relations is good boundaries. I have worked in very close teams and many times reflected on how well we got on with each other because of the respect for boundaries. What is included and what is excluded. It was a tacit agreement. Often in couples, the relationship deteriorates because of issues of boundaries.

Everyone has aspects they would like to keep to themselves. The betrayal of personal space is felt very acutely. It makes people react.

The difficulty is finding a balance with intimacy. At work, there is no implication that we should be intimate, and it is quite easy, with a bit of life experience, to know how far you should go for not intruding in someone's personal space. You are not offended if someone does not talk about themselves.

But for a couple, by the nature of it, intimacy and vulnerability are vital. If one feels that the other is withholding something, it is automatically a threat to the ego. As long as you both do the same thing, it is fine. Reciprocity is vital in any balanced relationship, in any transaction. When people perceive this reciprocity is not right, they start to disengage. The other partner has then to interpret that withdrawal by themselves. It takes the form of an investment. "I put a lot of myself in this relationship. Maybe I invest too much. I can't trust them. They are hiding things. I need to invest less."

Equally, almost everyone unconsciously puts barriers to any social interaction. It takes time to develop trust. Until then, the exchange is filtered through fears, uncertainties, and concerns. That happens when people ring your door, when a stranger speaks to you in a public space, even with friends.

We don't know people's intentions. Better be guarded. If you give a hand, they may take the arm. If we give them information, what will they do with it? We are fearful of people who overstep boundaries. They threaten the balance. Out of balance is out of control.

Now you can see how anxiety fits in. Is this relationship a friendly place? If your previous experience of relationships, of any kind, is that the bond and trust were weak, you will be more reactive. You would have to test it to know if it is worth investing in. This can be very testing for the other person.

This is the unconscious thought process of someone in a relationship when they come for therapy:

- Safety comes from trust.

- To know you can trust, you have to test.

- You can rely on the relationship because it survived despite ups and downs.

- Challenging is necessary to test that you can continuously count on the relationship.

- You treat it badly because it is solid.

- You know it is solid because you test it.

- You test it by treating it badly.

'Bad behaviour' to test becomes the basis of the relationship. When you do that, the past, present, and future are affected. You have evidence, real and imagined. It shows it was and is justified.

If the relationship is always stable, it is not tested. You can't be sure. So you need to be sure.

As my friend Kieron says: "life is an experiential process, and we get trapped in thinking it's a meaningful process."

Finding the rules of the relationship game is about finding out what each wants and needs, how it needs to be communicated, and why it matters. It can be adjusted to what both partners want. It can be total engagement and honesty, but it can also be at their own pace.

You have to figure out the game, the rules, how to win, how to lose, how to play it, and why.

It is not easy, as built-in to human nature, there is a need to cheat.

If you are in a relationship, have you ever had a conversation with your partner about the rules of the relationship you are both in?

Do you feel there is reciprocity, in terms of telling everything that is happening to you, or in keeping a secret space that is just for you?

You may also review a previous relationship, a romantic one, or at work, or in an association, and review it in terms of reciprocity and boundaries.

Projections

A client, Paco, could not deal with what his life had become. To add to the drama of what his life was as compared to what it should be, he had the certainty that everyone around him was judging him: comparing what he had become to what he should have been. He could see it in the look of his children and acquaintances. Their judgement compounded his distress and reinforced it.

As soon as we judge, we distance ourselves from what we criticise. We are not aware of it. Try it for yourself now, think of someone and judge them, "He is not good enough." Even towards yourself: "I am not good enough." You would feel that now there is more distance between you two. If you judge yourself, there is a separation that was not there previously, between a judge and the recipient of the judgement. We don't realize how judging affects and isolates us.

We find other people who make the same judgments. It gives a feeling of being together in our separation. We look at each other from our pedestals and are either amused or outraged at their ways of dealing with that separation. We judge that too.

In therapy, we work on and build awareness of what is happening. What is happening out there, and what is happening internally. They are two different things but are just expressed as one reaction. Something triggers their judgement, and people react like the little dogs you see in parks who react to every other dog. They may be insecure. They may be stressed. They react by barking at everything that comes nearby.

In the same way that the little dog reacts to another dog, you react to an idea, a person, or a task. It is a relationship between the subject and the object. How do you perceive the object? How does it impact you? How do you identify yourself? What is the relationship between the two? We have a judgement for everything. Sometimes with little control over being reactive.

When a man's eyes meet another man's eyes, they can react by "What are you looking at me for?" with aggression. So, there is definitely an interpretation of the world being an antagonistic place; someone looking at you is a threat. Or, it could be that the two of you smile and nod, and that is a world that is a friendly place where you acknowledge each other.

It is about noticing what is happening. Noticing your reactions and how you build the concept of someone. How you, as the subject, react to the object that you have created. We look at people, make a story about them, attribute qualities, and continue the story. You look at a woman entering the coffee shop. She is probably like this or like that. And we are right because the only evidence is the one we make up anyway. It is like a child playing with her doll and telling her what she did was wrong and how she is now punished. The child mirrors what they have observed, attributing characteristics and traits to things and people.

We project onto people. We do this all the time. Especially with the people that matter to us, our families and partners.

Think of the last time you cast a judgement on a person. You attributed qualities to them and got angry, made fun of them, or felt pity for them. It may have been when you were gossiping about them with another person.

Replay the instance in your mind. Notice how you attributed qualities to the object of your attention.

Notice your reaction.

Notice what is real and what is made up, the stories you told, and the relationship between the two.

You can do it with people, ideas, and situations.

Games

Most people are reactive to what happens in a relationship. This is why it is important to have a clear purpose for being in that relationship. It provides the supporting framework to come back to when it hits choppy waters. It maintains a stable direction, as in the promises two people make to each other during a wedding ceremony.

The framework is normally implied by the type of relationship: family, friend, couple, work, sport, or other activity. Boundaries can be trespassed when the relationship and framework are not explicit or mutually agreed, so conflict ensues. Partners would react to whatever is happening in relation to what should be happening. It makes them frustrated, angry, disappointed, or surprised and happy. What ensues is a predictable set of moves and reactions: a game.

It could be a game that both players are keen to play. Like on the day they get married and agree to the vows. It could be a game of learning together, supporting each other, of tolerance. If it is those values, it is an open game of talking to each other if things are unclear. It is the opposite of a reactive game of jumping to conclusions or finding evidence for beliefs we have developed by ourselves.

If the two players are bogged down in discussing the details of a situation and disputing what happened, they are no longer playing a win-win game. Unfortunately, it is what happens in couple therapy sessions. Truth becomes selective, the context of a loving relationship forgotten, and the direction the dialogue takes is rudderless.

It happens in parenting. A child starts an argument, "Yesterday you said I could watch this TV programme. Now you tell me to go to bed. Tom's parents let him watch the programme". A parent who doesn't get sucked into the argument remains clear about what they want. "Ok, they do whatever they want at Tom's. Here you go to bed at bedtime." It is easy to get hooked in by an argument and start to question yourself, "Am I a good parent?" "Should I be like Tom's parents?". Whereas if you are clear about the direction you are going in, you don't get distracted. Kids would push the boundaries. That in itself is a game.

In a couple, one partner may start by bringing up an unrelated fact or event. The other cannot make the correlation with the present moment and wonder about the intention. It's a game they are not clear about. Unless they address it, they become wary of the other's moves and intentions. It takes two to play a game, so maybe one may decide they don't want to play. In itself, that becomes a game, the game of frustration or non-participation, the game of withdrawing from the game.

People go for job interviews and don't know what's expected of them. It is a game where one party, the panel, is playing with rules they know, and the other, the candidate, is trying to figure out what they are. Candidates don't know how to answer. Whereas if they are given a specific problem for which they have experience, they know they could demonstrate their capability. The issue comes from playing the game without clarifying it. Frustration builds because of the uncertainty. Whereas if you could ask the interview panel what they are looking for and what level and degree of detail they want in the answer, the candidate could easily give evidence. Sometimes it may be intentional for the panel to be ambiguous to see how the candidate deals with uncertainty.

People even play those kinds of games with themselves. They don't know the intention, the rules, or the point of what they are doing. They get triggered and reactive by themselves. When reactive, they tend to do the opposite in reaction to something that dominates them. Sound familiar?

The only way to transcend this condition is to accept. Accepting is liberating. Otherwise, it is like being in a game without knowing it. Then you are stuck at a reactive level, this happens, and you react this way. That happens, and you react that way.

There is also the game of guilt: projecting whatever is happening and giving it meaning. Centring everything that happens around yourself. "This guy doesn't like me because he is looking at me." "She doesn't like me because she is not looking at me." The game is to find whatever reasons. It is a system that affirms itself. We project judgements on people and find all the evidence for it. She is not trustworthy. You find plenty of evidence. It may not make you happy, but it will make you right and make the other stable. They are good. They are bad. You know where you stand.

There is the game of arguing as a couple. What are the rules? How do you initiate it? How does it start? Continue? End? What is allowed? Not allowed? Included? Excluded? What moves are the players making? What buttons can you push to make the other player lose their stability or calm?

A common complaint from women about their man is that when they seek clarification about what is happening, he withdraws within himself. It makes the women even more in need of explanations and makes the man escape even more. They retreat into their mind cave. Not exclusively men, of course – I've seen that kind of avoidance in women too.

For many, having to perform when being with someone, entertaining, or justifying themselves is a domination.

In couple therapy, you often see both partners reacting like children. They lack a clear purpose, so they are easily distracted. They want to address problems but end up arguing, justifying themselves, and blaming the other. A mature couple would not have this drama. They would have clear principles. No distractions.

Throughout life, especially at the beginning, you have learnt rules about how to play the game of life. What to do, what not to do. You picked those rules from your parents, other significant people who influenced you, teachers, friends, and characters on TV or in books. You are unaware that the game you are playing now consists of predictable moves. So it happens that we naturally question rules, wonder about our life, and speculate about the rules that run them.

If you become aware of the game, you can begin to change it. There is the game you are playing and have not chosen and the game you can decide you want to play instead. Figure out the game you are playing and the rules you want to change. Look at it and add details to it. Unless you map it, you can't refine it. It is like the first time they made cartography. They sailed around Britain and had a general shape. Then as they sailed again around the island, little by little, they refined the shape, they got more detail.

> If you are in a relationship, it is worth discussing the game you want to play. As if you were to invent the game of football, or whatever game that takes your fancy, discuss your relationship as a game.
>
> What is the point? What are you trying to achieve?
>
> What are the rules?
>
> How do you know you are winning?
>
> What happens when the rules are not respected?
>
> Are there any breaks?

Contracting

By default, when you enter an arrangement with someone, there would be uncertainties about what will happen. The future is uncertain. There are always aspects that you can't predict. People are reliable based on experience, but not always. If it is someone you have never met, and there are stakes, you would somehow be wary of them. The brain is scanning for danger. You try to fill the gaps: Do they have a vested interest? What will happen? How? What if? What will you get out of it?

There is what you should do, and there are the unknowns. For example, I should talk to a builder about the kitchen extension, but I am anxious because it would mean dealing with builders. Several people have told me they are overbearing and unreliable. You have no way of knowing if they will do a good or a shabby job.

How do you reconcile being confident to make the decision and the risk of doing what you want?

By making expectations explicit to avoid disagreement and ensure that both parties know what is expected of them and what they get out of the transaction. So you create a contract. It can be a formal or informal contract, like between an employer and an employee, where some reciprocity or agreement is implied.

Contracts have several benefits. One is that they make the future known. You address what could go wrong, so it relieves anxiety. Secondly, clarifying aspects of the contract gives you confidence in the reliability of the person you are dealing with. Suppose the builder you have contacted and now talking to is very clear about what is involved. They would tell you what could go wrong and delay the work, the administrative aspects of the planning permission, and describe the sequence of what will happen in detail. In that case, it gives you confidence that you are dealing with an experienced professional. It builds trust. Thirdly, the way they treat you makes you feel adult and responsible. It makes you feel good about that relationship. If you can do that, there are other things you can do as well. It opens an all-new world.

However, people tend to be passive. Their anxiety surrounding these unknown issues prevents them from being active. They are not facing the problem because they are anxious. It is a coping mechanism. Thinking about the kitchen extension now automatically induces anxiety. They forget about the kitchen because they don't want to deal with builders.

You would have to deal with the external aspect, talking to the builder, and with the internal aspect, your self-management. You have to deal with anxiety. A female acquaintance had to take a car to the garage and pre-empted having to deal with macho mechanics who she thought would be condescending and con her. As a result, she got rid of the car and now takes public transport.

For some people contracting is the natural thing to do, whereas others would assume everything would be OK and that they don't need a contract. Even with yourself, it is particularly relevant. It is as important to be clear with yourself as with others. You need to know what you will put in and what you will get out. People are usually not clear about what they will get from doing an action. Or if they do, it is usually badly formulated. For example, you want to do an action, but you need to have confidence. Confidence implies you will get the outcome. You will achieve the result.

For example, when you want to ask somebody something, like asking them out for a drink, what's needed? Confidence. Where are you going to find this confidence? You can't go to Tesco and ask for a tin of confidence. Yet most people behave as if this is the case. They would say I don't have the confidence. And wait.

You do need some initial confidence to initiate the action, but most of it comes as a result of your actions. If you have done a challenging task, now you have the confidence. You have it as a result of that action.

If you are clear about what you have to do, what you will get out of it, and agree to the effort required, you have contracted with yourself. It gives you confidence and energy.

When something seems like a good idea, you get the feeling you would get from having done the action. It gives you confidence.

Contracting helps to stay on track. In the example of someone going to a party to meet people, contracting with oneself to remain curious about the people they meet would help remain focussed on the outcome.

When you contract with yourself, it helps to iron out issues that may come up, preventing you from deviating from your intentions. You are more together.

> Think of something you would like to do but see as a challenge. Acknowledge your reactions, feelings, and thoughts.
>
> Notice what you would need to overcome your reluctance.
>
> Think of what you would get out of doing the task.
>
> Think of the effort that is required.
>
> Now contract with yourself. You do this action, put the effort in, and you will get the outcome.
>
> Do you agree? Do you have an agreed contract?
>
> Next, initiate the action and notice how you feel about the effort.

The game of procrastination

We all have things to do that are a source of discomfort

and so we avoid them.

The point is to become aware of the pattern of avoidance. A reminder of its structure, as we have seen in previous chapters:

You should do something that you are not keen on

You feel the tension, the resistance to the 'should'

You want to avoid the domination of having to do it

You engage in escapism behaviour instead and feel relieved.

You could look at it as a game. You are playing against 'procrastination' who is running a scam against you. Become attentive to how the scammer operates.

Beware, it is not about getting rid of the procrastination, but seeing how it works; this will eventually change your attitude from passive to active. When you start to be curious about it, it will evolve. Otherwise, by trying to escape it, you reinforce the pattern.

Pick something that you procrastinate doing.

Observe the pattern operating with curiosity as if you were spotting a con.

> Become aware of the 'should > tension > avoidance of domination > escapism behaviour' pattern.

Good habits and attitude

So far, we have covered that life is stressful, and it is normal to be anxious. To avoid the unwanted feeling, we distract ourselves by engaging in various behaviours, some constructive, some detrimental. We described the different dynamics and incentives to keep things as they are.

We stressed the importance of recognising what was happening and accepting it.

Now we are going towards what to do, the good habits to develop and the right attitude to aim for. We will also cover the issues you could encounter when implementing new habits.

On breathing

A client arrived for a session. She was very stressed and borderline panicking. Rather than gauging the source of her stress, we worked on regaining control by noticing that she had control of her breathing. Then we moved on to noticing that she had control of her behaviour, like not only how she wanted to breathe, but how she wanted to stand and move her body. Once she realised she had control of her body, we moved to establishing control of her thoughts. As a result, without discussing what troubled her when she arrived, she left the session feeling that she was in control of the situation as well as her life, and could decide what she wanted to happen.

When people are in a distressed state, getting them to control their breathing is universally accepted as the most important way to stop their panic. It is a basic procedure well-known to firemen and nurses. Shallow breathing sets off your fight or flight mode, triggering the sympathetic system. In fight or flight mode, your body is ready to react. However, if you breathe deeply, you trigger the parasympathetic nervous system, the calming and reassuring response of the body system.

When appropriate, showing a distraught client how their breathing is unconsciously affected by their state and that they can consciously control the situation by regulating their breathing is very useful. Not only can they manage their stress through controlled breathing, but more importantly, realise that they are capable of regaining control of themselves despite their circumstances. "Take three deep breaths before you speak."

Having control runs through all aspects of life: getting back in control when something goes wrong, having immediate control of what comes next, and control of your actions.

Practising pursed lips breathing:

That is an exercise practised by nurses and other helpers to reduce stress and anxiety:

1. Take a deep breath, filling your belly, not lifting your shoulders.

2. Then blow out through pursed lips as if you were whistling or blowing air on your spoon full of soup to cool it down.

3. Repeat several times.

It has a relaxing effect on your nervous system.

Pay attention to what you do and the effect it has. It is the most important: associating what you are doing and the result. First and foremost, it shows that you're regaining some control.

Additionally, if you can, involve other senses. Imagine the sound of your tension being blown away, feeling your becoming grounded, as if you are landing, and seeing the tension leave with your breath, like smoke or mist.

Becoming aware of one's control reverses the vicious circle of stress. You are regaining control in order to become resourceful and building your resources to have more control.

That perspective stops you from being controlled by the actual problem.

Then you can do the same with those thoughts that are not serving you. You can disengage the autopilot and rediscover the joy of taking the commands.

Furthermore, when you are not able to face the demands, if you can't deal with the external world, breathing exercises are the best way to pump energy in your system. When you have energy, you have the power to make decision, to face the world, to express yourself with authority. 5 minutes of energetic breathing will do wonder.

Meditation

Our experience is always subjective. We have a blended subjective experience: a mixture of various inputs we get from our senses. It is evaluated in a frame of reference, our values, and we rationalise it in an objective understanding.

We have this relentless phenomenon of continuous recursive interaction between internal and external and have mostly no awareness of it.

We have a subjective problem; we try to apply an objective solution. But something is lost in translation. It doesn't fit. That is the crux of the matter. We try to run the show, and when we stop and accept that it doesn't work and become a detached observer, and stop trying to make something happen, there is room for reconciliation between those two aspects. It is where meditation helps.

In itself, the practice of meditation encompasses everything that I describe in this book, especially dealing with distractions. In life, there can be tension and anxiety about what is coming next. You get distracted until you bring your attention back to what is happening and being mindful of your experience at that moment.

Even if you are aware that you are thinking, you can recognise it as a fact. "I am having thoughts."

However, especially for beginners, trying not to lose focus is difficult. They stress because they are not supposed to have thoughts, and yet they do. Because you can't help it, thoughts come. You should not be thinking about things and lose your attention, but you do. It creates tension and, therefore, more thoughts, such as comments on what is happening. Now you have an irritating commentator describing your performance.

Meditating is supposed to be effortless, but you can't help trying hard. The mind is agitated. Thoughts come and go. We usually can't dissociate from our thoughts. Your thoughts are your reality.

Some people are adamant that meditation is not for them. It causes anxiety, and they can even become agitated if they persist.

For one thing, there is a lack of stimulus. Some people find silence very uncomfortable because it lacks the normal background noise that they are used to in their daily lives.

This background noise is their routine and it is reassuringly familiar. It allows them to be in the 'can mode.'

We also attach many meanings to the noise around us: it symbolises life's hardships; it signifies belonging to the world of busy people with a lot to do; and it gives sense to tension. Some people can't stop and take time out. They can only relax by taking on a different type of tension.

Many people find pleasure in thinking ideas, or being in action, which give them a sense of achievement. Doing nothing as meditation is perceived, being passive i.e. not actively thinking and not physically moving, is counter-intuitive for such people.

The other aspect is the domination of the idea that they should meditate. They were told it was a good idea. However, the more stressed they are trying to do it, the worse they feel, and therefore they react against its domination.

There may be a combination of reasons why they struggle.

However, if you are satisfied with your meditating, you are in control. You have regained control. You don't have to meditate. You can get the same benefit through other activities you have chosen, like listening to music, playing an instrument, or crocheting. As long as you know you are doing it for the purpose of focusing your mind.

In meditation, when you reach a deep level where there is no more reactivity. It's like listening without any noise, seeing in ultra-sharp definition, and being able to feel out rather than reacting. It allows for deep concentration, easy, calm creativity, and wise intelligence.

It can be pleasant to be in relationship with yourself, your inner self, and turn off the commentaries. some deep truths that you may have not listened to can come up. Whether pleasant or not. It can feel like when you are on holiday, and able to reflect with what is happening in your life, or like being with someone special to you.

There are many forms of meditation, but mainly it is being quiet, either still or in movement.

I will describe a traditional sitting meditation. It would be common to Buddhist or Christian ways or any other denomination.

Start by listening to the sounds around you. Close your eyes. Hear the sounds as input, as if you would listen to the soundtrack of life. Both the internal sounds you generate and the external sounds. Don't judge or try to identify them, whether you are attracted or want them to go away. Let them be.

You cannot help but identify them and be affected by their meaning. If you catch yourself doing that, let it be. The idea of meditation is to be a detached observer. Your thoughts are 'a happening'. You notice them as objects, as the noise of life, as if you were watching passing clouds.

They may capture your attention but when you notice them, let them go.

Don't judge your performance of detachment.

It helps to have a point to anchor your attention. Put it on your breathing, without putting any tension on your attention, notice breathing happening.

Somehow you are doing it, and it is also happening on its own, like your ideas. You are producing them, and they are also passing by as if you are not producing them. They come to you. Little by little, you discover that both are happening. You do, and it's being done. With time you will notice it doesn't matter. Breathing becomes a soothing rhythm, and you can notice that you are both doing it and not doing it. That process of observation without tension will lead to peace, a contentment with what is.

When meditating, you practise seeing what is happening as just a thought, an experience, not reality. It is the aim, depersonalising all that is happening in your mind and body.

So that you can take this ability outside the meditation in active life.

Put a boundary to this exercise. Find a space for meditation and a time for it.

Do it for 20 minutes and if it is too long, do 5 minutes. Or 2 hours. Do what you can.

Trance and awareness

The purpose and process of trance are similar but more active than meditation. Trance is also about a change in the nature of the relationship between subjective experience and objective understanding.

Trance is an everyday life phenomenon which occurs when your attention is taken by a thought or something happening, real or hallucinated, and you detach from your current reality.

It helps to explore options and scenarios without the inhibitory aspects of censorship that occurs in normal consciousness. It is like a daydream. You can daydream of relaxing in a pool, with a glass of champagne, in good company, without any concerns that you have no holiday allocation left and can't afford it.

At its most basic, intelligence is the ability to connect elements together as a whole and see the recursive causes and effects in a complex system. Einstein was famed for his ability to imagine the connections from what is to what could be, like imagining his theory of relativity, for example. To do that, Einstein would play the violin. This activity would help him release the tension created by the need to solve the problem. Buddha talked about attachment as a source of suffering. Attachment is tension. Pain is tension. Without tension, the problem structure loses its rigidity. That is why some people would think of a specific problem when they go to bed and wake up in the morning with the resolution. During their sleep, they have relaxed enough so that the problem has reorganised itself. The tension of the waking state prevented that.

Hypnosis is effective for that very reason.

Self-hypnosis is a form of trance that is dynamic, similar to meditation, but with a purpose more guided than relaxation. It is more directed towards achieving an outcome. For example, it could be to relax or solve a problem. It helps to release the tight hold of how we see a situation.

Trance can be induced by someone else. That is the role of a hypnotherapist. They would control your attention through relaxation and distraction so that they can direct it to where it is useful. They would facilitate your ability to focus. It can be to allow an experience, seeing things from another perspective, either somebody else's, to understand another point of view, or in time, like revisiting the past or jumping into the future to experience the consequences of what you do in the present. You can do that without hypnosis, but hypnosis makes it easier and more vivid. It can help in rehearsing action in the future. It can remove the restriction of normality, like distorting time or space, and disconnect meanings. It releases the limiting tension.

The reason for discussing trance here is that trance is a rehearsal. When you rehearse, you come as close as possible to the real thing. When you rehearse a performance or explore various scenarios of cause and effect, as in how people could react if you say this or that, you make what is unknown more known. When you do that, you reduce the anxiety of the unknown. You permit yourself to try different 'as if scenarios' and choose what suits you.

Planning the future

Without conscious consideration, the future resembles the past. There is no reason why it shouldn't be the case. If you are happy with the way things are, that is fine. Life, in general, is about replicating itself. Nothing has to change if you are satisfied with the past or the present. Tomorrow will take care of itself.

Many clients are unable to stay focused on what is happening now. They have a compulsion to talk about the past. They may be stuck because something is unresolved. So they see a therapist to resolve what is uncompleted.

And because they can sense that it is working well, they start thinking about the future. But if they have not something there, if it's empty, it spooks them, so they disengage from therapy.

The place where there is nothing more to complete about the past and nothing to think about in the future is unbearable. So they stop and drift away, back to their usual life of suffering. Without a future, the dynamic aspect of life stops—depression, melancholy or relentless crises follow. When people would like to think of the future, and nothing positive comes up, they go back to the past, which is known, and generally purged of bad memories. They get occupied in the present, in avoidance mode, which means mainly doing trivial activities to stay occupied.

During the 18th and 19th century industrial revolution, life changed and created a lot of stress and uncertainty. Life as people knew it was disappearing, so they reminisced about the Middle Ages, chivalry and romanticism. They thought of that period as a better time. Literature and art from the Victorian period found inspiration in the idealised Middle Ages. Walter Scott would write Ivanhoe, and the pre-Raphaelites would find inspiration for their paintings from medieval Arthurian legends.

Experience not only gives you knowledge of what will happen but most importantly, in the context of anxiety, it tells you what is not going to happen.

We think of an activity or a task, and if we don't know how to accomplish it or what the consequences will be, we stop. We procrastinate or decide that we don't want to. "It's too complicated to get there. I won't go. I'll stay home instead". We would need to think through an activity or task to connect to what we will get out of it. When connecting to the good feeling of the outcome, we are motivated. "Sophie will be there? I like chatting with her. I will go". The benefit is worth the cost. So you act.

Through experience, you also learn that things will get worse, and so the need to act will come, and you may as well act sooner rather than later. For example, you are too shy to ask where the toilets are, but as it becomes urgent, you come to a point where you ask. You get the answer and feel good because you have overcome your shyness and will satisfy your need. If you learn quickly, next time around, the time it takes to reach the threshold is reduced. You will ask earlier.

It may be worthwhile to consider that things will get worse. If you don't learn, you don't progress. For most of us, the default setting is safety and comfort. Until the need to do something becomes urgent, we don't act. For example, "I am relaxing, taking it easy at home, but if I don't go to the shop before it closes, I won't have anything to eat for dinner." We can foresee the consequences and therefore only have to deal with laziness. For more abstract things, such as dead-end jobs or relationships, it is more difficult to foresee the consequences, so we avoid doing it.

The quality of life, its comfort, depends on learning. Replicating what works well and not replicating errors. And both success and failure can be learning opportunities.

The size of the action you have to take is also important. You need to be able to measure your progress and be motivated to do more. If it is too ambitious, if you take too much on, you will experience anxiety and go back into your shell. So, to build your comfort and confidence, you need to take baby steps. It will help keep your balance and spur you to increase your step naturally, without forcing yourself. You would go into excitatory mode rather than inhibitory mode.

It is equally true with physical activity as it is with thinking. When you go at your own pace, without the pressure to achieve something, you activate your excitatory mode. That means you become inspired and start to generate ideas, and be creative.

Anxiety comes from anticipating negative consequences in the future. We are anticipatory in how we live life. We live now to build our future, whether for the next five minutes or life in general. In case of something negative in the future, we feel angst and avoid that event to avoid that anticipated bad feeling. By avoiding, we feel good because we have acted by avoiding that danger. On the other hand, if we look forward positively to an event that we decided we want to happen, we feel good in anticipation and act to make that future happen.

There is a right balance to strike between not planning because you don't want to feel dominated by plans you know you are not going to fulfil, and having plans that cause you to act now, something that calls you into action. Automatically if you have a future that is bright, that you can grasp, you like the idea of, and start to take action, your outlook on life changes. It raises your energy.

There is a need to be complete about the past. You can be angry or sad about the way you have been treated unfairly or tossed some bad cards in life, but not at the expense of spending the rest of it being stuck. If you are, it may be because you don't have an exciting enough future, a compelling future that makes your present dynamic. A future that gives it a sense of direction. Otherwise, it is a static present. Having a present with a purpose, or a present connected to the future, gives you a sense of purpose and belonging to the context of your life, to your reality.

When you make plans in all areas of your life and start acting to realise your plans, you feel good. It's energising because things are as they should be. You now have a purposeful to-do that takes care of your anxiety.

> Do you spend more time thinking about what you don't want, ruminating on the same old complaint, or do you spend more time thinking about what you want and how to make it a reality?
>
> Consider your life at the moment. How much is it orientated towards the future?
>
> Are you more in avoidance mode in general or curious, positive, keen to manifest?
>
> Do you have projects that call you forth?

The important aspect is to pay attention. Make it a regular practice.

If you regularly pay attention to your mood and attitude, it will reveal the beliefs you have about the future. People naturally rehearse the future, mostly out of awareness, and play out worst-case scenarios that scare them, so they stop and go back to distractions to avoid the anxiety.

If you think about the future and what you experience is anxiety, you are facing a lack of resources or an oppressive demand. Are you acting on whichever seems the one you can do something about? Otherwise, wishful thinking is not going to change anything.

About intentions

An intention, a belief, or a new habit you want to have, is like a baby.

You may be very happy when they are born, but for them to survive, they need to be nurtured. You need to treat your intention like you would a baby. Care for it regularly, feed it, stroke it, speak to it. Those repeated actions would make you bond with your intention, like they would with the baby. You have to regularly be with your intention, at least daily. Imagine it as it is happening now. Immerse yourself in the situation, and involve all your senses. Either visualise it or narrate it to yourself, or both, depending on your natural abilities, and put as much emotion as you can into it: what you feel, what it means to you, what you are proud of. Take various perspectives, from your own eyes, and from an external perspective, like from an observer's.

Like you would for a baby, you need to make room for your intention. It needs to have its own space where it can grow. So you have to think about where your intention is going to grow and how it is going to fit in your system.

How does this intention currently fit in your life context?

What adjustments need to be made?

Do you need to make it a priority, like a mother would with her baby?

Do you need to plan time, and fit it into your schedule?

A contribution from NLP (Neuro Linguistic Programming) that students value is that of the logical levels, devised by one of the pioneers in NLP, Robert Dilts. Aligning those levels would help integrating the intention in your life.

Consider each of those levels.

Environment

What is the context of that new intention? If it is for example doing exercise, that would be the state of your body and fitness. Externally it would be where you would be doing the exercise, who with? A class? In a gym? By yourself with a website? More generally what would be the current state of affairs where that intention would fit?

Behaviour

What would you be doing? What would be the sequence? Imagine yourself doing the behaviour.

Capability

How would you be doing it? Do you have the skills needed? That is where the baby steps are important as you may need to build your capability.

Values, beliefs

What do you value about this intention, what do you believe about what is associated with it? What are your reasons for engaging in this activity?

Identity

What kind of person does what you intend to do? Is it how you see yourself or could see yourself? How would you see yourself? What would be the perception of others about you?

And beyond that, your mission, your purpose: What is this intention part of? What would be the implications of doing what you intend? Why does it matter? Why do you it for?

Finally, a baby needs time. You may have the intention to go from a to z, but be patient. You may need to break it down into baby steps. If you try to go faster than the time needed for the full maturity of your intention, it will spook it, and you will have to be extra careful because your intention would now be wary. Take your time.

Purpose

The subject of finding your life purpose and being on purpose is a popular one. It is usually stated as a statement of intention, like "I want to save the world," "help the poor," "fulfil my potential". It is usually derived by looking at what is important about what we enjoy doing, particularly if we feel alive when we engage with it. Our purpose can also be arrived at by a realisation emerging from a crisis.

Often though, striving for a goal is maintaining an unconscious awareness that something is lacking. For example "I want to make money, be rich". It becomes a solution that maintains a problem – being poor. The solution presupposes the problem and the problem has many negative implications. When we think about them and we feel bad. The solution is a reminder of the problem: i.e. "I can't look after my family". Guilt can sneak in and undermine that goal. "I want to be rich, I am a failure." Then you may find yourself not doing much to advance that goal. For example, you are in a relationship with someone. They have undermined your trust because they have done something behind your back. Any projections or plans to do with the future are difficult because now you don't trust them. You also feel bad because you stay with them. The problem is that you don't want to be alone. Your purpose to be in a good relationship is not fulfilled.

The danger is when the purpose and the everyday reality are disconnected, as we described earlier with mission statements, usually about how important customer service is to an organisation, where there is nothing in reality that relates to that intention. It produces only a feeling of betrayal and cynicism.

In life there is continuity, but us humans jump from experience into concepts. From the concrete here and now, the thinking can become abstract and detach from reality. We then go from territory to map. It happens when we think of what we are doing or what is happening is part of something bigger, a classification, when we generalise, or when we listen to someone else's point of view. And we are not aware that we do that. If we were, most problems would disappear.

We are not there yet and have the illusion that we will be. If, despite our efforts to fulfil that goal or purpose, we don't have a sense of progression, it will reinforce our impression that something is inherently wrong. You may have observed people addicted to self-development courses or preaching to others what they should do, being the most deluded and unfulfilled people.

Finding your values and purpose in life is like finding a partner. What matters is the relationship the relationship to your values and purpose. Most people feel like they lack direction or purpose. Not because they don't know their values or purpose but because they don't know how they live and experience them. So they slowly fade away.

Sometimes, it is not so much getting the outcome that matters, but the connections and learnings you get along the way. It could also be why. Why having this purpose matters. It is important to review the integrity and well-roundedness of that purpose. If it is just a good idea but disconnected from your reality, it will lead to disappointment. What is most important is to have a feedback mechanism to notice when you are on purpose and when you are not. If you have feedback that you are on track, you won't get lost and will create a virtuous circle.

Living a life where we ongoingly feel that we fulfil our values or serve a purpose is empowering and rewarding. An exercise well worth doing. If you can live a life that serves a purpose, it will be a fulfilling life.

Goals and purpose are worked out in the map, particularly to plan how you will get there. But the living of them is in the territory. You need to measure your progress both on the map and in the territory, get some feedback in reality.

Are you clear about your values and purpose? Does it matter to you? Why or why not?

How do you keep track of where you are in relation to your purpose?

Emergent quality

The need to reciprocate can get in the way of appreciating a gift you have received. What is true in relationships with others, is true to the relationship to life. When we are caught in a vicious circle of cause and effect, we try to cause something as a means to an end. We expect a result, and we tense because we depend on that result. That tension is not conducive to finding fulfilment in the outcome. A much better approach is to create the conditions for the result to emerge. For example, a guy is trying to impress another person and is being perceived as such, which is referred to as coming across as needy. Whereas when someone is enjoying doing something without an end outcome in mind, the energy it communicates is congruent. It communicates relaxation and a positive attitude. It is natural and belongs to the context.

When you are attached to a result, you are in cause and effect. There is an inherent should. There is tension because a part of the system doesn't belong and wants to.

One of the most popular talks on the internet is that of Carol Dweck, a Professor of Psychology at Stanford University. She approaches this area in her own way. She proposes two types of mindsets: a fixed mindset and a growth mindset. A fixed mindset, in relation to achievement, is based on character traits, such as "You are successful because you are intelligent". In the case of a growth mindset, success is attributed to the efforts you have put in. The difference in how pupils perform in education with the two systems is well documented. If they are praised because their success is based on the fact that they are intelligent, they have to consistently perform as one at the top. They live in the anxiety of what could happen if they fail, which inevitably would happen at one time or another. And when they fail and don't live up to their standards, it is an upset.

Whereas a student who is praised on their efforts, regardless of the end outcome, is motivated to put more effort in. And when you put more effort into studying, it is more likely that you will get a good grade on the exam. It doesn't cause it directly. You may study hard, and the questions are not related to what you have prepared for, but it increases the likeliness.

A good farmer looks after his land. He works at nurturing the soil. It doesn't guarantee a good crop, but it helps. And in doing so, he feels good that he is doing his part. The plants' business is to grow. And life's business is to provide the weather. Regardless of the result, the farmer is aware of the boundaries of his control over the process, such as adverse weather conditions, and can be at peace with himself.

Surveys done in the workplace show that employee satisfaction and a happy workforce are not based on external incentives, such as bonuses, but on the intrinsic value found in one's own work.

As with my example of gluttony for ice cream, the point is to develop awareness of the 'can mode.' It is not about changing the behaviour directly. Awareness brings the condition for change to emerge in the same way that children stop sucking their thumb or pacifier by observing other kids around them in kindergarten. It works because of emergence. Clients change in therapy because they evolve.

Therapists just create the conditions to do so. They help to increase the client's resourcefulness, reframe the demands, and change perspectives.

That is also how Toastmasters work. Toastmasters is an organisation that promotes public speaking. Members are not taught public speaking; they just practise talking in front of others. Improvement emerges from observing others praised for what they did well and given ideas of what else they could do better. What goes for public speaking goes for life in general.

Are there aspects in your life where you are more in cause and effect mode, and others where you are more into creating the conditions for the result to emerge?

These may be the same area, but the emphasis would be different.

Identify them.

Harmony

People have their own way of doing things. It is their own culture. It has developed organically. What works for them doesn't work for others.

Problems start when people follow a method that is the latest trend; in dieting, they do low carbs, low fat, or intermittent fasting. It either works for them or not. Others follow the ideology behind it, like vegetarians or vegans. They don't just do a diet. They are vegan.

You either belong to whatever system you have chosen, or you don't. If you don't, sooner or later, a part of you is going to rebel. It is not going to work long-term.

Following others' solutions often leads to the creation of problems that did not exist. Most of our skills should grow organically. It is the principle of apprenticeship. You start to become more competent at what you do, and new learnings integrate into the system. You have time to adjust at your own pace. It is connected to that principle of continuity, between territory and map mentioned in the previous chapter.

When what you should be able to do, or know, is dictated by an outside source, problems start. It is no longer based on your needs but on someone else's. "You should buy our product" (and the need you didn't know you had will be solved!). It can also be dictated by you to you. "You should go on this course or this workshop." "You should be seen with those people."

You think of changes you need to make, which are external, instead of the transition to adapt from where you are to where you want to be, which is internal. You need time to develop existing skills and integrate them into your know-how. But when it is a solution to something wrong with you, dictated by should, it creates issues.

Disharmony can happen between the mind and the body. For many people, it is not going to bed when they are tired. When we resist something and persist, we become ill or experience pain. Exercising is a good example.

One day, I met with a friend at a swimming pool. At the time, I wasn't doing any physical exercise. I was unfit. On both those days, I swam 50 lengths, a total of 100 lengths over two days. If I had pushed myself, I would have subsequently been in agony. My arms, legs, back, and neck would have been in pain. But I was absolutely fine in the following days. I swam and focused on feeling good doing the movements. I swam at a good pace but was very mindful of what I was doing. I didn't impose a task on my body. I didn't try to reach a goal like many people do in gyms or when running. They do it violently, as if they have to tame their body and beat it into submission. The mind dictates, and the body has to follow. But then later, they are in pain. That did not happen to me when I did my lengths.

Similarly, you may have heard stories of children that have only ever eaten cornflakes all their life or some other restricted diet. I met a boy who just ate chicken. That's all he ever had. That's all he liked. He looked fine. It may have consequences later, but he had done it for 14 years without apparent issues. A friend of mine fasted for a week then started eating moderately afterwards, and he did not go back to binging. He had not deprived himself and now needed to catch up, like many people do, as if they had withheld their breathing and were now gasping. He has practised doing all kinds of endeavours effortlessly in a belonging state. The mind behaves in the same way as our immune system. What doesn't belong is rejected. Life works when we are in a belonging state.

With clients, harmony is arriving at a stage where they can manage what is happening externally and what's happening internally. In other words, how they manage what's happening in their interactions with the external world and their response to it. They can take some distance. They are able to make choices and decisions and accept their choice. They can do that in a balanced way. They are mindful of their needs and that of others. They accept that doubt will always be there, that they will always be questioning themselves, and that they have choice. They remind themselves that they have been in similar difficult situations before, and managed.

They are used to the tension of dealing with life, recognising that it is necessary to be who they are. We are like the strings of a violin; if too tight, it's not right. It doesn't resonate as oneself. And if it is too slack, it doesn't make the right music either. So, to be in harmony with oneself, one always has to have tension created by things you question and anticipation of what's next. By doing so, you are tuning into yourself. You adjust the tension with the right amount of 'is' and 'should'. You tune by acceptance. When you accept, you can see that you are what you are, and take it with compassion and humour. If you don't accept that, you become a drama queen who is insufferable to yourself and to others.

If you don't take time to reflect on what's happening, rather than get carried away with what's happening, you are at the mercy of external circumstances. You are always reacting to things happening out there. You want freedom from something instead of freedom to do something and take responsibility. There is little room to be creative if we are reactive to what's happening out there. To be creative requires a certain amount of relaxation, enough tension and relaxation. There will always be in the environment something that makes us tense. Many would say it happens when they go to their family, where they regress and react like a child or teenager. The feeling of domination trumps taking responsibility for things to be as they are.

When you feel it's enough: "I don't want this automatic reaction to everything that is happening," when you don't want to be reactive any more, when you want more meaning, you may start to see signs. It is often represented in stories as the archetype of returning home: we discover that the answers we have been seeking outside actually are inside.

The archetype of the hero's journey is of going out there, into the world, and finally coming back home, to the truth. The mind is like the hero; it meanders, gets lost, suffers. When it gets back internally, it comes back to simplicity, discovering the beauty of simple things. Letting go of the tension linked to complexity and relaxing in simplicity.

Teaching people to be happier is often helping them become more aware, notice, appreciate and have gratitude for what is. It requires slowing down. Often when we are caught up in the whirling of life, we are going at a pace that is not in our control, but we get used to it. We need that speed to feel exhilarated, alive, like on a roller-coaster, especially youngsters. It is addictive. And when we slow down, that exhilarating feeling is missing. It's not right. Like if I go out on Saturday night, go home, and still have adrenaline in the system. I can't go to bed straight away. I may watch TV for a bit to make the transition. And then it is back to normality.

What happens when we are going fast is that any decision we have to make becomes significant. Imagine being on a bike or any vehicle at speed. If you have to make any decision, you have to react quickly. It's binary, do this or that. There is danger in making the wrong decision. You're under pressure, tense, you are dominated by time pressure. It's this or that, dominated by the decision to make. No time to think. The wrong decision, and you crash. It can be as exhilarating as it can be frightening. Additionally, there may be a need to raise energy and be more decisive in many contexts. Fast pace adrenaline is an addiction.

Whereas when you can slow down, when you are not under pressure, what you thought was mutually exclusive, is now possible to consider.

In most situations where you are under pressure, if you could remove the time factor out of the equation, the domination would disappear. That's what you do naturally when you procrastinate. You forget about the deadline, and the pressure disappears. Not always, but in some cases, you can choose to remove the time factor. Often people feel bad about something they have to do because of a self-imposed deadline. For example, a client wanted to tell their parents about her partner and thought they would not approve of it. We agreed that maybe one is never quite sure about a relationship. It is subjective to say you are sure. That meant she was not in a rush to tell her parents yet. That removed the need to act, to have to tell. Even though, in reality, she is sure, but it is acceptable to give time before having to act.

Take a context where you are in flow. All is well. You are in the 'can mode.' It can be being with friends at your local pub. It can be walking in your favourite spot. It can be being in your comfortable chair, listening to your favourite album.

When you have your example, consider that all the elements belong to the context. They are in harmony. It feels good.

Surrender

When clients are improving or have resolved their problem, they let go of the tight grip they had on being right about a situation, about their beliefs, or opinions. The tension has lessened, and they can now think and feel differently. A sense of renewal and possibility is now available.

The two main forms of feeling bad, the two forms of not accepting what 'is' for what 'should be', are sadness and anger. Sadness, in its worst expression, is depression. Depression is a closing down of the external world, a folding in on oneself. It is the progressive alienation of the self from the external world. The person isolates in a bubble, where judgements about others and the world are generated by the self without any validation from outside. They judge and give themselves a sentence, like a judge would do to someone who has done wrong. Depressed people know that they are responsible for their pain. They are the judge and the convict at the same time. Depression leads to becoming more and more self-centred. Whereas happiness and presence are focused on the external, or being aware of the system and our place in it.

Anger, and the tension attached to it, are also about the self. It requires being right against the outside world being wrong. It prevents surrendering to life and the magic of being alive.

Water is a good example. If you fight against it, you end up tired and drown. If you stop fighting and relax, you float.

Happy, enlightened people, or those following a spiritual path, surrender to something bigger, whether it is God, life, or energy. It is about going from the self, me, or ego to a bigger scope, belonging to something bigger, with humility. It implies the same process of acceptance, of letting go of being right and stuck, to what is useful, what works, and is harmonious. It is the space that a therapist should provide.

If you consider right versus useful, right is centric on a position. Useful is going beyond. There is movement. In the same way that fear is contracting, a reaction of the self against the world, love is an expansion, a movement outwards. That transcendence is the general direction of life.

Generally, people strive to be successful. They are focussed on themselves. They get older, retire and give the rest of their life to the good of the people around them. They can even look after the grandchildren in a more relaxed way than when they were parents. They become more altruistic or do charity work.

When you are young, it is natural to take things personally. When you are old, it is time to learn to accept. But you don't have to wait to be old to get wise.

You need to embrace your negative aspects, what you don't accept about yourself. Otherwise, you maintain the tension.

Can you make the difference between giving up and surrendering?

Think of examples in your life where you gave up on what mattered to you and ended up diminished, less alive.

Now think of examples when you have surrendered and felt a release of tension and fared better.

Existential considerations

People reconsider what matters to them through becoming more mature. So our values change with time. But it can also be triggered by some traumatic event: the upsetting of a routine, the tragic loss of someone or something that mattered, or a brush with death.

Have you ever had a spouse or partner who told you the relationship was over? They found somebody else, or maybe they moved on. Maybe you were made redundant from a job, and it was unexpected; or even earlier in life, if you can remember that far, the loss of your beloved teddy bear. Something important to you vanished. That changed everything. This disruption of knowing what reality is, perhaps something you have never had to think about before, can create existential angst, the unpleasant feeling that maybe life has no meaning or purpose.

Existential angst arises from the void created by assumed truths that evaporate or from the doubt that what you knew to be true, and have taken for granted, is not. And you wonder what else? What else do you believe to be the case is not? Where else do you delude yourself?

You come to realise that you had the misconception that you were in control and that you are not. You want to take back control, and paradoxically, you know that ultimately you are not in control. It is all futile.

So, what does this mean? What to think of it? Knowing that the structure of your reality is an illusion, that life has no meaning.

Knowing that there is no meaning can bring humility. This is the condition for accepting what is.

But we can't help but try and make sense of everything. We create meaning for everything that is happening around us—even insignificance.

What does it mean that there is no sense? That what happens in life doesn't mean anything? You get stuck in an existential vacuum, feeling empty and aimless. Nothing is connected; it is chaos. It can lead to depression.

Other people would instinctively rush to your rescue to feed you meaning:

"It was not the right girl/guy for you, she/he didn't deserve you."

"With your skills, you will find a job easily."

There has to be a meaning.

Philosophers have continually reflected on the lack of meaning or the creation of a meaningful life. The existential quest for life having no meaning requires us to find a way to accept it and be at peace with it. Or on the contrary, we can focus on following a doctrine, a philosophy, a religion, an order, a system of values and rules, something that gives meaning to life.

To take an aspect, meaninglessness or meaningfulness, and to analyse it without the context of the two existing as a system in equilibrium does not make sense, as in Yin and Yang. They are both there, life with a lack of meaning or life with meaning. But people side with one or the other, or one against the other. It would be like saying that inhaling is what matters or saying that exhaling is what matters.

Indeed, life has no meaning. You could see it as a succession of things happening, and yet people need to create meaning. We can't help it. And when they're fixated on making sense of life, they need to realise the futility of wanting to make sense of it in a rigid way.

Relax...

Just remind yourself: we attach meaning to everything, even when we try not to. Yet, in themselves, things are meaningless. It is what it is. And yet, you can't help but

Regain control of your life

make it mean something. So just pick a meaning that is generous and kind to yourself and others.

You can do this exercise within the scope of your life, or if it's too ambitious, take an aspect of your life. For example, the status that your work gives you.

To begin with, use what we have practised before, which is to put yourself in a state of relaxation, to be present and at ease.

Think about the status your job gives you. Accept that it doesn't mean anything, that you can let go of what it means. It is just something you do.

Then, once you've done that, think about why this job gives you status and all that is connected to it.

Once you have considered each of these aspects, switch from one to the other several times: accept that it doesn't mean anything and that it is very meaningful. Back and forth.

When you can do it with one aspect of life, do it with life as a whole. Everything life means, what it is all about, and that life means nothing and is a continuation of things happening. Switch back and forth between those two beliefs a few times.

Develop your best state

If one's body is too acidic, it would be a terrain conducive for cancer to grow. In the same way, a tense body resulting from an anxious mind is going to be a fertile place for reactive or negative thoughts.

Your state is the environment in which the thoughts are produced and what kind of thinking takes place.

Bad stress accumulates. Even when released, too much stress cannot be eliminated, like sugar turning into fat. It is not because you stop that the effects are eliminated. They stay in the system for a while, and stress transforms into physical symptoms, from allergies, and skin conditions, to cancer. The system reacts against the stressor, sometimes by self-destruction. Too much acidity in the body is too much stress for it to cope with, and it cannot maintain healthy homeostasis.

There is a delay between when you stop the unhealthy habits for the effect to take place. The same goes for stress. People are surprised when their health is degrading. They may have forgotten they experienced stress a while back.

Often you have to keep going when you are stressed. In the same way that if you were chased in the wilderness, you would be stressed and pumped up with adrenaline. It is afterwards when adrenaline and cortisol have dropped that you would feel the effects. That is why when you realise that you are changing, give room for blips. Just notice that you are generally better. It is not linear but a succession of ups and downs.

With less stress, you can deal with what is, rather than perceived threats. You can't take more in a tense state, only protect yourself. The external world becomes a threat because you cannot cope.

Being calm and relaxed in some situations is a useful point to start with, but in others, the best state could be more dynamic: calm but excited. Relaxed but ready. It depends on the context and the demands of the situation. Everyone has a state where they are at their best. A way of being that is optimum. The important point here is to become familiar with that state. Pay attention to it and cultivate it. It is the state of mastery. Masters, in whatever discipline, would be focussed but relaxed. Each would have a different level of energy which is the ultimate one for them to excel. Finding yours could be one of the most important searches in your life. It's what every performer aims at. Think of times when you were at your best, in the flow of life, and felt great. How did you stand? How did you breathe? How did you feel?

What about your energy? Do you feel like you have mastery in the context you are in?

Think of that state. Feel it. Adjust it until you get it to a satisfactory level for the task at hand.

Practise it so that it becomes your default setting.

Start with specific contexts. What is the best state to be in when you are about to speak to others? What is the best state when you are about to start exercising? And during exercising? What is the best state when you plan your day?

That state is when you can stretch boundaries and remain relaxed. It is what you would do and experience in yoga. You stretch and tense but in a balanced, controlled way. You can maintain a pause that causes stress, but that stress is OK; it belongs, it fits in. You don't fight it or push it away. It is about body-mind connection. You can find it in sports, dance, or any other activity where there is pressure in a controlled way. When you are at the peak of your performance and yet remain unstressed, you will be in what is called a flow state. It is not limited to those areas. Any physical activity where you are responding to what is happening, with a sense of knowing what you are doing, where you are experienced, would be it. It is achieved without the mind interfering. The best state is in the 'can mode.'

Pick something you do, an activity that you enjoy. It can be digging potatoes in the garden or serving at tennis. Pay attention to the state you are in.

Pay attention to all aspects: the way you stand, breathe, the tension around your eyes.

Cultivate that state. Observe and nurture it.

Next time you engage in that activity, put yourself into that state before you start the activity(in fact, that process happens naturally, but you could willingly expand it to other areas).

You can do all that in real time when you do this activity. You can do it now, in your imagination.

Life's demands

Sometimes you may like to rest, and you have to continue. The demands at work, at school or at home are relentless, never ending, you would like to stop but you can't. Life prevents it. Emotionally it translates as feeling dominated and either feeling sad, angry, depressed, tired or numb.

By contrast, being asked to rest when we want to be active is less current, but many people experienced this during the lockdown. It could give us a feeling that we are not used to our potential. It affects our relation to ourselves and how we judge and treat ourselves.

I have covered state in a previous chapter. We are now going to look at the importance of energy. When you grow old, it is more apparent. It determines what you do, but it equally affects you throughout life.

Our thoughts and how we feel make us act a certain way, reinforcing how we think and feel. We are tricked by the drama of life. It is difficult to escape this conditioning. It is natural that we can't dissociate from our thoughts. Our thoughts are our reality. When it,s a beautiful day, we feel happy. But when something bad happens for which we take responsibility, we identify ourselves as a failure. Our body is deprived of energy, mind and body are depressed. Our experience is us. Manipulating reality would be compromising our identity.

People do try. They know "fake it till you make it." They try to be congruent, but it is to achieve a result. They are aware of their manipulation. Reinforcement of helplessness and demotivation follow.

The ability to resist temptation is related to your level of energy. When you are low, you are more likely to let yourself be tempted or swayed.

When you are feeling better, you can try to let go of the bad habit again. Applying what was described previously, the gearbox model: acknowledge it is not working, accept that it is not working, agree to give yourself space, and decide what you will do next.

If you are too stressed, it may be difficult to do anything. There are times when you feel down, so you think down. It is not the time to make decisions. Just know that you are down and likely to have down thoughts, and it's not the time to plan. Postpone until you are back to your resourceful normal state.

As an illustration, I had a call with a friend who had a frustrating day in relation to a project she was working on. She was feeling despondent and tired, it was late, and she had a conflicting debate with herself. A whining voice that was in tune with how she was feeling was telling her that maybe she should give up and forget about her project. So, she felt tired, sad, depressed. I advised her not to listen to that voice, to postpone any decision until the morrow. Otherwise, it would be like listening to a young child who is cranky, tired, and whining. The best thing is to put them to bed and have a good rest; tomorrow is a new day. I advised her to do a pleasant activity for 15 minutes she was going to listen to music and go to bed. The day after, she was back on track and happy she didn't make a rushed decision about her project.

When you are in a period of constant demands, exceeding your resources, your energy fluctuates. When you are depleted, ideas and moods are more likely to be on the pessimistic side. Your current state is used to assess how you will be able to deal with a demand. It's more difficult to think about your capability to do a task unless there is an external spur. That external spur could be a commitment, like a meeting or a piece of work within a deadline, which would surpass how you feel.

A person used to being self-motivated is not taking low energy well. They push even further with the little energy they have. It is a question of personality, as we have seen with the Transactional Analysis Drivers in the chapter on Resources and Demands.

Whereas as you grow old, you get used to the little amount of energy available to you during the day and appreciate it. It also dawns on you that striving for more, a better life, a better body, or self is the source of unhappiness. Maybe it is about stopping striving for a better reality by finding your own meanings and sense of purpose and finding happiness doing so.

When clients are down, defeated, and depressed, they can barely think of solutions and be positive. The lack of energy makes deciding difficult. Risks are amplified. That is when getting guidance, counsel, or ideas on what they should do from someone else may not help. The helpers consider the situation from a normal state of self. Clients are not their normal selves. Helper/advisors are unencumbered with ambiguity. They propose a way forward in abstraction to the rest. The person in the problem, however, has lots to consider, including that they don't have the energy to address what they should do.

When you are tired and have to perform a task, either under an external constraint or by pushing yourself, you quickly feel dominated, so you tense. When you tense, you become reactive. Being reactive leads to few choices and a lack of control. You may want to avoid the pressure, but maybe you have to get on with it. This process becomes a downward spiral. All the aspects I describe become more acute. It can lead to burnout or depression. There is no more energy, now and in the foreseeable future.

When you assess a task, no matter how simple the task is, you compare your level of energy to the demand of the task. Usually, you would do the task if you had a sufficient amount. It's Sunday morning, you get out of bed, and you see you have to clean the kitchen as you hadn't the night before. You take in the state of the room, which means the amount of energy it will require to sort it out. You check how you feel. The idea of doing it tires you. Better have a coffee and breakfast first. Hopefully, it will boost your energy. Afterwards you will be able to clean the kitchen. Several things may happen simultaneously:

- The food is transformed into energy, and you feel better, more energetic.

- You feel good because you rewarded yourself with the breakfast and now feel in a good mood to do chores.

- The tension you felt when you presented yourself with the task for which you didn't have the energy has now been dissipated. You got used to the idea and you are relaxed about cleaning the room.

It's important to point out that it is perceived resources, not objective.

It is easier to raise your energy, or calm the system than change bad thoughts or negative thinking.

Over time, it is also useful to know how you function. So, if something happens, you have learnt how you function in that situation. It is useful to consider various factors:

- What fatigue or energy state was I in when this and that happened?

- What time of the day?

- How much sleep did I have?

- When did I eat last?

- How fit am I?

- Did I exercise recently?

- Are there any other contributing factors?

Positive states come from maintaining good habits. It is worth considering the environment, the light, the noise, the social aspects, validation, or your insulin level. They would dictate and may be more important than your trying to understand the problem psychologically.

The pain of doing something new can be overwhelming. When you have built a life of avoidance, it can be difficult and appears impossible to change that, and to a certain extent, why should you? Avoidance can be the way of solving problems, and anything different will make you react. When you are used to the life of comfort and tolerance, you can easily push away the memory of the other life where you had ambitions and goals.

The curse of man is to forget because they grow habituated, because of the 'can mode,' and because they move on to other activities that keep them busy and take their attention away. You may need to re-experience the cost of your current situation to spur you to move. However, it is always important to have a way forward if you do that. Do not throw yourself in the pool if you can't swim.

Let's take the questions I proposed in the chapter about your condition in a situation where you did not perform as you normally would or when you failed. Think of the example before you ask yourself the questions below.

- What energy state was I in when this and that happened?

- What time of the day?

- How much sleep did I have?

- When did I eat last?

- How fit am I?

- Did I exercise recently?

- Are there any other contributing factors?

Creating a virtuous circle

When the external conditions are not great, it is a good idea to find peace in your mind. You can only find peace when you accept what happens. Humbly, responsibly, accept. I don't mean tolerate. I mean, don't try to deny reality. Whatever you try to accept, there are often aspects that you can't accept, what should not be. That is what you need to accept. What should not be, is.

Wherever you are in the process, remember to take baby steps. Acknowledge the little steps of progress.

For example, if something would normally make you angry, notice that you are less angry. Noticing that you are less angry than you would usually be is progress.

Sometimes from where you are to where you want to be is unrealistic, but there are steps in between that would be more doable. For example, I don't believe I will run a marathon by Christmas. But I can believe that I could start running once a week, once around the park.

Come back to the awareness of creating a positive feedback loop. Pay attention to getting what you thought you would get from something. For example, if you thought that a walk would make you relaxed, when you come back from the walk, notice that you are relaxed.

Do that for all your intentions. Life would improve as you practise being and maintaining living in a virtuous circle. You would be calmer, more fulfilled, and happier. When you are generally happy, in harmony with life, all seems to belong. It all fits together. In the same way unhappiness and discontent breed more of it, being willing and positive opens opportunities. Start your positive feedback by doing one thing now. One that you find pleasure in doing, appreciating as you do it, and feel good having done it.

When you are in the state of relaxation and are at one with life, that is the time to practise integrating into your life things that still seem to be a challenge and where there is still resistance. Utilise what was covered in the habituation chapter: Have a sense of yourself being contented. Pull the idea of that challenging thought, the object, into your 'contented space', or, if you want to let go of something, someone, a habit, do the opposite and make it go away slowly. If you start to feel resistance, move the object of your thoughts back where it feels ok until you are ready to start again. If the resistance persists, spot the thought that is in the way, and apply the same process. Move that thought away whilst you are serene. Then initiate the first step of the action you want to take. And as you are in the action of doing what you previously struggled with, focus on maintaining that softened state.

You can apply that process of habituation to the concepts in the book. The most important thing is to know and believe that a method is right, and when you fall off the path, give yourself some slack and go back to applying the advice. If you are convinced that it works, go back to it. You need the evidence that helps you believe it is right for you. You need to be convinced; otherwise you will continue to search for an elusive alternative and fall for the next tempting offer, another method, another book, another video on YouTube.

What often happens is that we come across an idea, a method or a piece of advice that sounds good. It fits in your map. But you don't apply it. It does not transfer to the territory, so it fades away. And you go from one idea to another, endlessly, feeling good when you find another idea, but overall frustrated because there is no concrete difference in your life.

If you find an idea that makes sense, you need to apply it to make it yours. You need to practise it regularly until it is second nature; until it becomes unconscious and is sustained by the evidence and satisfaction you find along the way. In the same way that starting to run whilst unfit is painful, but when you are fit, there is no effort and only pleasure.

This can be done with someone not feeling in control of what is happening in the moment, and it is a good practise to do with yourself.

If you develop this ability, you can apply it to many contexts where you would like to choose how things are happening.

Wiggle your fingers in front of you. Then move your hand, and rotate your wrist like a dancer. Then move your arm and the other. Stand up if you were sitting, and start to sway, still moving your arms, hands, and fingers.

Notice that you can decide the speed, the energy, what to do next. Notice that you are in control. Put it to your attention that you are completely in control of what you are doing, that you can choose. Notice your stance and your attitude. Take this stance and attitude to what you do next.

Gratitude

At some level, all problems come from missing information.

What are the implications of not having the information you need? For example, what will happen to you if you lose your job? Who would you be able to count on? What will happen to you and your family, if you have one?

A sports team manager may say to his team, "the opposition is stronger, so don't worry about losing. Go and enjoy yourself. Play your best game." The underlying assumption of not knowing what would happen, the uncertainty that creates anxiety, is replaced by the certainty of knowing they are going to lose. They are free and often produce greatness.

Gratitude is an example of being active, creating feedback that would not automatically be present. What others would take for granted, someone who practises gratitude or acknowledgement is being active in creating feedback in the system.

Gratefulness tends to generate more gratefulness. In the same way as when we are with friends and start thinking of anecdotes from the past, we generate some more anecdotes. You have to start with what you have and be grateful for it. It reconnects you with a sense of belonging with those aspects and helps to extend to other things you can be grateful for.

Pick something in your environment, an object you can appreciate and feel grateful for, then move on to something else, like another object, picture, or souvenir.

If you can't find something to be grateful for, you can acknowledge that if you are not connected now, you were in the past. There was a time when that object meant a lot to you, and be grateful for that.

I was keen to start exercising a few months ago. I could be grateful for having the intention, and reconnect to a sense of belonging to fitness and good health then, and wonder if it is still the case now.

If you can't find anything to be grateful for because you feel bad, you are true to your feelings. So you can be grateful for being true to your feelings.

What's next?

Now that you have read this book, and if you find value in its ideas, put some of it into practice and read the book again. You will discover some new connections each time you do so. Every time you apply something new, it opens the space for more to learn.

I have experienced it whilst writing the book. It became an opportunity to try some of the advice in new ways. For example, I could not sleep at night, always thinking about what to add to the text and what order to put things in. It prevented me from sleeping, not because of stressful thoughts, but because my brain was overstimulated. That is when I started to apply what I suggested in this book: acceptance of what was happening: the sleeplessness, mixed with a sense of being alive, excited, feeling good. Then I noticed the distinctions of the 'can mode' (pleasure in doing, availability and permission). I deliberately noticed feeling alive, good and peaceful was available. It felt good. I would encourage and give myself permission to continue to indulge in that state.

It was a state of surrender, close to the one you reach in deep meditation, where you have profound truths, yet you are neither attached nor excited. It is similar to being in a meadow, surrounded by beautiful flowers, without having the need or the impulse to pick them. You can just be there, appreciative.

You could try it for yourself now. You don't need to do formal meditation. Just make yourself comfortable and generate that feeling of feeling good; notice that the positive state you are in is available and pleasurable, and give yourself permission to be in it, ongoingly. Whilst in it, you can start to add movement. Feel your connection with the space around you. If you like the movie Star Wars, make it 'The Force'. Then all your fears and negative thoughts can be 'The Dark Side.' Surrender yourself with that 'Force' space and start to bring your life into it. Bring the things that mattered to you in that bliss.

Learn your limits and become sensitive to tell-tale signs. What happens in that state: acceptance, light, love, presence, belonging, connection absence of tension, judgement, should, comparison. Become familiar with it so you can recognise and access it more easily and recognise when it is not happening.

When you know that you are able to generate that state at will and have a bad thought, it does not escalate into more thoughts because now you have a choice.

Knowing that you have choice stops the rumination of negative thoughts. You can reverse it by looking for choice.

May you use it...

In the 'can mode' chapter, you have learnt about the components of pleasure, availability, and permission. It happens when you do something habitual when you don't need to think about it. It's unconscious.

What would happen if you did that consciously?

What would happen if you became conscious of the pleasure, availability, and permission aspects of what you were doing and started paying attention to the effect?

Become aware of your state, of what is happening now. Mix it with a sense of being alive and feeling good.

Then notice the distinctions of the 'can mode'.

Feeling alive, good, and peaceful is available; it is pleasurable.

Encourage yourself, proactively give yourself permission to continue to indulge in that state.

Make it a practise that becomes second nature.

Finally, remember that what you have to accept is that nothing lasts. Tomorrow will bring a new challenge. What you think you have mastered is going to be tested. You cannot control what is happening in life, but you can control how you deal with it.

Having read this book, you understand how anxiety works a bit more and are better equipped to deal with it and what to do to alleviate it.

About Patrick

Patrick Baron is a professional therapist who has been successfully freeing clients for 30 years from a wide range of psychological and behavioural issues.

Born in Lille and now based in London, he works with clients both face to face and online. He is passionate about travel, cultures and figuring out how things work, including your mind. His style is informal, friendly and pragmatic.

Personally, Patrick embraces meditation and the principles of Buddhism and is a bilingual speaker of French and English. Professionally, Patrick has trained in various psychological and coaching models including NLP and Developmental Behavioural Modelling and he is a qualified Cognitive Behavioural Hypnotherapist

Patrick also has experience of business, having worked in recruitment, management development training and in the areas of change management and cultural transformation. He is a president of a public speaking bilingual club: Experience French Toastmasters.

Patrick is well travelled and in his spare time loves to capture the beauty of nature with photography. He is curious about what is happening in the world and in the mind.

You can contact Patrick directly to find out more about his therapy and counselling services.

07957 661887

patrickbaron@gmail.com

www.ingramcontent.com/pod-product-compliance
Lightning Source LLC
Chambersburg PA
CBHW021910040426
42447CB00026B/976